HITTING
IS NECK UP

The 90% Softball & Baseball Players are Missing

By Rogerick A. Thompson

Published by Rogerick A. Thompson
Madison, MS

ISBN (Paperback): 979-8-9943420-1-5

For information, permissions, or bulk orders, contact:

Email: Swingrxhittingllc@gmail.com
Instagram: @swingrxhitting

X: @swingrxhitting

Printed in the United States of America

10 9 8 7 6 5 4 3 2 1

COACH DISCLAIMER

This book is not a system, a checklist, or a substitute for coaching judgment.

The concepts presented are intended to inform decision-making, not replace it. Player development is contextual and dependent on variables that include, but are not limited to, the athlete's physical profile, perceptual skill, competitive level, training environment, and timeline for readiness.

The examples, frameworks, and illustrations in this book reflect tendencies and principles observed in competitive environments where performance is measured by production and evaluation, not intention. They are not meant to be copied or universally applied without consideration for the individual athlete in front of you.

Coaches are encouraged to assess, adapt, and integrate ideas in a manner consistent with their role, level, and responsibilities. Ultimately, development must serve the player and the game, not the framework itself.

Responsibility lies not in having answers, but in knowing what the game is asking and whether the athlete is being prepared to meet that demand.

ACKNOWLEDGMENTS

This book is dedicated to the two bookend men in my life. My father, who asked if I wanted to attend a Delta State baseball camp in the summer of 1989, the summer this passion first took root… and my son, RJ, who reignited that passion years later and has kept it growing, season after season, year after year.

To my wife, thank you for your unwavering support, patience, and belief. None of this happens without your steady hand behind the scenes.

To Dan Papizan and Rodney West, thank you for the coaching opportunity that transformed me from a swing movement specialist into a true hitting instructor.

To William Cook, your advice to "keep my eyes open" before I jumped into this rabbit hole became one of the best lessons I've ever received.

To the Lee Family and the Johnson Family, thank you for your trust when no one else was willing to give it. When everyone else were laughing, together we were learning.

To Perry Husband, the discoverer of effective velocity, who has provided clarity and understanding of timing.

Lincoln Martin, Josh Johnson and Kris Jenkins, the countless conversations that have been nutritional to my growth.

To Ryan and Harry Porter, our meeting at Pitch-A-Palooza opened doors that changed everything.

To Samantha Ricketts providing me experiences to make the connection between lower level and higher levels below the surface.

To Jeff Hargar, J.T. D'Amico, Chris Malveaux, Bryce Neal, and each of you have contributed how to look through multiple lenses for player development.

To Jim Best, thank you for the teaching environment of exploration and education for myself and players.

To Corey Dickerson, thank you for challenging me from the highest level of play, both during and after your MLB career.

To Corey Ray, thank you for the perspective of a seasoned professional player and coach.

To coaches who generously gave their time to share what they truly value in their players at the Mississippi High School Activities Association – Baseball (MHSAA), National Fastpitch Coaches Association (NFCA), American Baseball Coaches Association (ABCA) and Pitch-A-Palooza; your insight helped shape the perspective behind this work.

God places people in your path to help you grow.

Each of you provided the right nourishment at the right time.

For that, and for what this journey has become, I'm deeply grateful.

TABLE OF CONTENTS

FOREWORD - SOFTBALL

Some coaches come into your life for a season. Others change the entire trajectory of your career. This book is written by the latter.

I started working with Mr. Rogerick Thompson when I was fourteen years old, long before I truly understood what it meant to be a student of the game. Over the next decade, he taught me far more than how to swing a bat. He taught me how to think, how to adjust, how to trust myself, and how to compete with confidence. Everything I know today about approach began with him.

We are both, in many ways, hidden gems. We come from Mississippi, where softball is not always recognized or played at the highest level. Opportunities were limited, and belief did not always come from the outside. Still, we believed in each other when many others didn't. That belief, paired with relentless work ethic and a shared commitment to growth, became the foundation of everything that followed.

What makes Mr. Rogerick special is not just his knowledge, but the way he teaches. He is deeply passionate about his work and always explains why instead of simply saying, "do this because I said so." He leads meaningful discussions about hitting, understands the balance between the mental and physical aspects of the game, and helps players take ownership of their approach. Even as a great teacher, he has always remained a student of the game, continuously learning, growing, and connecting with some of the greatest and brightest minds in baseball and softball to better himself for his athletes.

He helped me tremendously throughout junior high and high school, but his impact became even more meaningful during my collegiate career. When I had drifted away from some of the things that once made me successful, he helped me return to them. He reminded me of what I did well, helped rebuild my confidence, and challenged me to improve in areas where I could be better. From ages fourteen to twenty-two, he has watched and nurtured my growth and development as a player in the game I love.

This book is for coaches, players, and anyone interested in growing in the game of softball or baseball.

The lessons shared apply at every level and across all backgrounds for those who are striving to compete at a high level. My career is proof that the approaches in this book work. Using these principles, I have experienced success at the highest levels of collegiate softball, including First Team All–Big 12, All–Big 12 Tournament Team, Second Team All–Pac 12, Third Team All–Region, and Pac 12 Freshman of the Week honors.

This book represents many of the things discussed in our decade-long, growth-minded partnership rooted in belief, curiosity, and love for the game. If you are willing to learn, think deeper, and trust the process, the lessons in these pages will meet you where you are and help you grow, not just as a hitter, but as a relentless competitor.

Alana Johnson

2023 Women College World Series - University of Washington

2025 Women College World Series – Texas Tech

FOREWORD - BASEBALL

I knew Rogerick was a phenomenal baseball mind from the very first question he asked me. We had just met, and while I was still playing, he simply asked what pitch I was hunting for in my next at-bat. I'd talked to plenty of fans on the on-deck circle before, but Rogerick wasn't a fan he was a student of the game. Curious, thoughtful, and always searching for deeper understanding.

Every conversation I've had with him, I walk away having learned something. This book is no different.

Rogerick isn't your typical hitting coach. Yes, he can get into the weeds with biomechanics, but what makes him special is that he values what matters even more; approach, preparation, and how a hitter actually competes. He doesn't try to give everyone the same swing. He teaches hitters how to succeed with their swing, equipping them with a plan based on how pitchers will attack them.

As a former hitter, I can tell you it's a lot easier to hit when you understand what's coming. Rogerick teaches hitters how to do that. Not by guessing, but by building an educated approach that tips the odds in the hitter's favor.

Whether you're a coach, a player, or a mentor, reading this book will make you better. This isn't just instruction; it's the product of a lifelong learner sharing what truly matters.

Corey Ray

Washington Nationals – First Base Coach

INTRODUCTION

WHO IS THIS BOOK FOR?

A Note Before You Begin

> This book will not give you all the answers. **Instead, it will challenge how you think about hitting and equip you to discover your own answers**.

Why? Because every player is different. Different bodies. Different timing systems. Different movement patterns. Different learning languages. Different strengths and vulnerabilities.

A systematic answer that works for one player can destroy another. A cue that unlocks one hitter can imprison another. A mechanical correction that helps one athlete can create barriers for another. My job isn't to tell you what to do. My job is to help you discover what works for YOU, or for the unique player you're coaching.

This book is designed to assist players and coaches in coming up with individualized answers, not to deliver universal solutions that ignore your uniqueness.

> If you're looking for "the system," you won't find it here. If you're looking for the questions that lead to your answers, keep reading.

1. THE CAGE STAR WHO CAN'T PRODUCE IN GAMES

You crush in batting practice. You look beautiful on video. Everyone says you have a "pretty swing." But when the lights come on and the pitcher starts mixing speeds and locations, something disappears. Your confidence evaporates. Your timing falls apart. Your production drops.

You know you're better than your stats show. You can't figure out why your cage performance doesn't translate to game performance. This book will challenge you to ask: Am I practicing the right things, or just the comfortable things? Is my swing the problem, or is my approach the problem? Do I understand myself well enough to articulate my strengths and weaknesses?

This book will help you discover why cage bombs don't equal game production, the difference between swinging and hitting, and how to assess what YOU do well versus what the system says you should do well.

2. THE TALENTED PLAYER WHO PLATEAUED

You dominated in high school. You were one of the best in your state. You got recruited to a good college program. Then you arrived on campus and everything changed. The pitching got better. The competition got tougher. Your weaknesses got exposed. And now you're sitting on the bench watching players with "uglier" swings produce while your "perfect" swing collects dust. You keep working on your mechanics, hoping something will click. Nothing changes.

This book will challenge you to ask: Was my high school success built on inferior competition or genuine skill? Am I working on what needs fixing, or what feels comfortable to fix? Do I know myself well enough to communicate my needs to my college coaches?

This book will help you discover the difference between corrections and compensations, why your "perfect" mechanics might not fit your body, and how to become the player who understands themselves on Day 1 of college.

3. THE COACH WHO KNOWS THERE'S MORE

You've coached long enough to see the pattern: The players with the best mechanics often have the most inconsistent results. The players who "see it and hit it" sometimes outperform the players who drill positions endlessly. The talented player struggles while the less talented player thrives. You know there's something missing in your instruction. You know mechanics aren't the complete answer. You're not sure what the other piece is.

This book will challenge you to ask: Am I teaching hitting, or just teaching swing? Am I forcing players into my system, or adapting my coaching to their individuality? Do I know the difference between my biases and their needs?

This book will help you discover the missing 90% that determines success or failure, how to assess each player's unique strengths and vulnerabilities, when to correct, when to compensate, and when to leave well enough alone, how to communicate in each player's connection language, and why some of your "best" coaching advice might be creating barriers for certain players. You have very little time to teach them from the neck down. You may provide your player with hitting wisdom not provided outside of your program.

WHO THIS BOOK IS NOT FOR

This book is NOT for you if you think hitting is all about mechanics and bat speed, you're satisfied with cage bombs that don't translate to games, you're unwilling to question what you've been taught, you believe your system works for everyone, you think elite players just "figure it out" on their own, you're looking for a quick fix or magic drill, you want one-size-fits-all answers that don't require thinking, or you're uncomfortable with the idea that your beliefs might be wrong.

If that's you, stop reading now. This book will frustrate you. Because this book challenges everything the hitting industry has told you. It questions the biases you've accepted as truth. It exposes the clichés that sound good but produce nothing. It demands that every player be seen as an individual, not processed through a system. It requires that you think differently than you've ever thought before.

THE JOURNEY AHEAD

Here's what you're about to discover:

CHAPTER 1: THE SWING VS. HITTING - Why beautiful mechanics aren't enough, and the painful lesson a high school softball player taught me about the difference between swinging and hitting.

CHAPTER 2: CAGE BOMBS AND HARD TRUTHS - Why feel-good training leads to game-day failure, and what 10-year-olds taught me about real hitting development.

CHAPTER 3: THE THREE PILLARS OF A HITTER - Decision, Discipline, and Damage, the three elements every elite hitter possesses and most good hitters are missing.

CHAPTER 4: BEYOND BALL EXIT SPEED - Why your $17,000 technology might be working against you, and why the phone in your pocket could capture more useful data.

CHAPTER 5: FINDING YOUR STRENGTHS AND VULNERABILITIES - The assessment system that reveals your actual strengths and weaknesses (not what you think they are, but what they really are).

CHAPTER 6: MECHANICS, RHYTHM, TIMING, AND PATH - When to fix and when to compensate, the most important decision you'll make as a hitter.

CHAPTER 7: THE ART OF HUNTING PITCHES - Why hunters dominate and reactors fail, and how to become the predator instead of the prey.

CHAPTER 8: DISCIPLINE AND EXPANDING YOUR ZONE - The strike zone prison you didn't know you were in, and why your hitting zone might not be the strike zone.

CHAPTER 9: MAXIMIZING YOUR LAST FOUR YEARS - What college coaches wish high school players knew before arriving on campus.

CHAPTER 10: HITTING BIASES AND BELIEFS - The invisible cage made of beliefs, and why the barriers you can't see are the ones destroying your development.

WHAT MAKES THIS BOOK DIFFERENT

This isn't another book about swing mechanics. You won't find detailed kinematic sequence breakdowns, ground force mechanics diagrams, the latest trendy drill that "unlocks" power, or a systematic approach that works for everyone.

Instead, you'll discover why Ted Williams was right about the 50% — in many cases, I feel as much as 90% — and what that actually means for your development; how to identify your true strengths and weaknesses using simple methods, not expensive technology. Why "all strikes are not equal" is the most important concept you've never been taught; how to hunt pitches with intention rather than react with hope; the difference between your strike zone and your hitting zone, and why it matters; when mechanical work helps you and when it hurts you; how pitching coaches scout your weaknesses and how to prepare for their attack; why the prettiest swing often fails against the best pitching; and how to build an individualized approach that works for YOUR body and YOUR timing.

THE PROMISE I'M MAKING YOU

I can't promise this book will make you a .400 hitter or produce them. Nobody can promise that. But I can promise this: If you apply the principles in this book, you will understand yourself better as a hitter. As a hitting coach, you have a framework for identifying and addressing real problems, approach competition with intention rather than reaction, and give yourself the best chance to be consistent against quality pitching. As a result you separate yourself from coaches or players who only know how to swing, and be equipped to discover your own answers as a player or developmental methods as a hitting coach.

More importantly, you'll understand what Ted Williams knew 55 years ago: Hitting really is at least 50% from the neck up . The question is: Are you ready to start training the 90% you've been missing?

A WORD OF WARNING

This book will make you uncomfortable. It will challenge some beliefs you've held your entire career. It may question coaches you've trusted. It will expose biases you didn't know you had. It will reveal that some of the work you've been doing is actually working against you.

You'll get angry. Angry at coaches who focused only on mechanics. Angry at instructors who gave you cage bombs instead of real development. Angry at the industry that sold you the 10% while ignoring the 90%. Angry at yourself for not questioning it sooner. That anger is good. Because anger leads to change, and change leads to breakthroughs. But only if you're brave enough to face uncomfortable truths.

THE CHOICE

You're standing at a crossroads right now.

PATH 1: Keep doing what you've always done, Work endlessly on mechanics. Chase perfect positions. Hope talent is enough. Wonder why results don't match effort.

PATH 2: Train the 90%, Start with the mind, not the body. Question every bias and belief. Hunt pitches with intention. Break free from limitations you didn't know existed.

Path 1 is easier. It's what everyone does. It feels like progress. But Path 1 leads to plateaus you can't explain, talent that never translates, and potential that remains unrealized.

Path 2 is harder. It requires honesty, self-awareness, and the courage to train differently than everyone around you. But Path 2 leads to breakthrough performance, confidence under pressure, and maximized potential.

Which path will you choose?

HOW TO USE THIS BOOK

This isn't a book you read once and put on a shelf. It's a working manual for player development.

FOR PLAYERS: Read it through once to understand the concepts. Then revisit specific chapters as you encounter challenges. Use the assessment tools to evaluate yourself honestly. Apply one principle at a time rather than trying to change everything at once.

FOR COACHES: Use this as a framework for individual player development within your team system. Not every concept applies to every player, but every player needs to understand themselves. Consider how you can create variety in your lineup rather than uniformity.

FOR PARENTS: Read this to understand what your player should be working on beyond mechanical drills. Use it to ask better questions of instructors and coaches. Most importantly, use it to help your player develop self-awareness.

LET'S BEGIN

Somewhere right now, a talented player is in a cage working on their swing. They're focused. Determined. Convinced that more reps will solve their problems. What if their problem isn't their swing at all? What if it's that they're working on the 10% while ignoring the 90%?

It's time to discover what hitting actually is. And it's not what you think.

"The fascination with swing mechanics continues. Still hidden and not found: the fascination with hitting." Let's change that. Turn the page, and let's talk about what Ted Williams knew, and what you need to discover.

Welcome to the 90%.

Before You Begin

They polished your swing until it gleamed,
Then wondered why you never dreamed
Of pitches hunted, not just seen,
The cage taught nothing in between.

The prettiest hardware, silent mind,
Three pillars you were taught to find

Too late, Decision, Discipline, Damage,
While coaches spoke a foreign language.

Exit speed won't save your soul
When you don't know your striking zone,
When vulnerabilities unnamed
Leave you guessing, getting blamed.

They never said: *Don't chase the ball.*
They never said: *Know when to stall.*
They drilled positions, perfect form,
But left you naked in the storm.

So here's the truth they never taught:
The mind decides before you're caught
Between the pitch you think you see
And the hitter you were meant to be.

Mechanics live from neck on down.
But hunters wear a different crown,
They know the zone that's *theirs* to own,
And swing at what they've *chosen*, not just *shown*.

Your last four years won't wait for more
Of what the cages had in store.
The biases, beliefs, the lies,
It's time you learn to trust your eyes.

Ninety percent. That's what he said.
Ted Williams knew: *It's in your head.*
The swing's the car. The mind's the map.
Time to wake up from the trap.

CHAPTER 1

THE SWING VS. HITTING

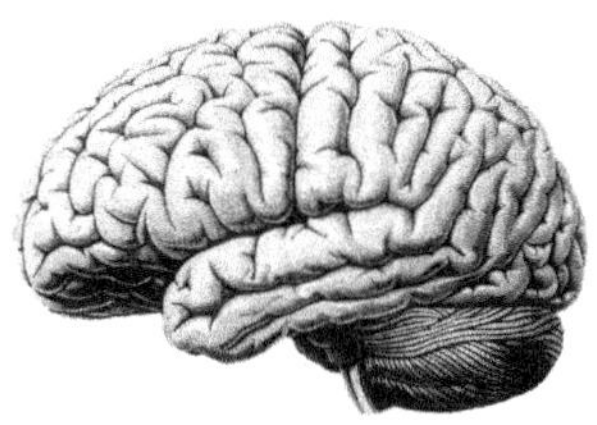

The Hardware of the Swing and Software of Hitting

"The prettiest swing in the cage is worthless if you don't know what pitch to swing at." - Coaching wisdom

I turned my son into a swing robot. From age 7 to 14, I dragged him to cages applying all the newest information from some of the highest-level clinics in the country. I studied the biomechanics of the swing. I analyzed swing videos frame by frame. I flew to Colorado for a specialized hitting certification. Read tons of books and subscribed to several online products.

I attended Pitch-A-Palooza, ABCA, NFCA, and On BaseU workshops. I read The Biomechanics of the Baseball Swing until I could recite it. I became obsessed with perfecting his swing, his load, his stride, his rotation, his bat path. I became very knowledgeable about the swing, yet I never once taught him how to hit.

I didn't even realize there was a difference until 2017, when a high school softball player taught me what a decade

of coaching clinics did not discuss on stage: The swing is your hardware. Hitting is your software. I'd been missing out on what really matters when softball players and baseball players step into the batter's box. How sad. We were informed of this over 50 years ago!

THE 55-YEAR-OLD TRUTH WE KEEP IGNORING

Ted Williams hit .400. No one's done it since 1941. In 1970, he wrote The Science of Hitting and handed us the answer: "Hitting is 50% from the neck up."

Read that again.

The greatest hitter in modern baseball told us the game happens in your mind, not your muscles. He was telling us about software, and we responded by upgrading everyone's hardware.

So here's the question: If hitting is up to 90% mental, why do you spend 90% of practice on mechanics?

In reality, in most cases we spend 100% on hardware, the body, the movements, the positions, the mechanical patterns. We obsess over what the body does and completely ignore what the mind decides. By the way, you can't include talking to players. Talking and teaching are not the same. Only consider practical application of approach training, game planning and adjustability!

HONESTY MOMENT

Stop for a moment. Think about your last ten practices. How many minutes on swing mechanics? How many minutes on decision-making?

Do the math. It tells a story you might not want to hear.

EVERY HITTER TRAINS HARDWARE. ALMOST NONE TRAIN SOFTWARE.

Ask any player what they worked on this offseason, and you'll hear the same answers:

"My swing."

"My mechanics."

"My strength."

"My bat speed."

These things matter, but they're hardware. They're the physical components of performance: the body, the patterns, the movements, the strength, the timing systems that the brain stores and executes automatically.

But elite hitters understand something deeper: Hardware doesn't run without software and software doesn't install itself.

To this day, most players work backwards. They spend the entire offseason upgrading hardware and enter the season with no software update. They train swing, strength, mobility, mechanics, exit velocity. All important. But when they step into the box in February thru May, they're running last year's software.

The brain is ready. The body is ready. But the mind is untrained, unclear, and sometimes completely unprepared for the decisions the season demands.

This is why so many hitters look great in training and average in games. Their hardware improved. Their software didn't. The two aren't synced.

When software and hardware don't match, the hitter underperforms the work they put in.

I was one of the worst offenders, honestly. When my son RJ started playing baseball at age 6 in 2010, I had dreams, the same dreams most dads have. I'd ensure he applied "my" knowledge of hitting and become the superstar every father imagines his son becoming. I used my experiences from attending Delta State baseball camps in 1990 and 1991 as a high school player, thinking I had all the answers for him and his teammates from the recreational league through high school.

After all, those experiences made me better. I was teaching him to upgrade the car and not how to drive it!

"Game day isn't the test track. There's traffic, weather, unexpected turns. That's when navigation matters more than horsepower."

DISCOVERING THE HARDWARE (AND MISSING THE SOFTWARE)

At age 11, RJ was directed to a local instructor who analyzed his swing and pointed out enhancements via slow-motion video. As a very technical person, even to this day, that was one of the most impactful moments of my educational journey. The seed was planted. The curiosity about this magnificent task of the swing was heightened.

One weekend, after reading The Biomechanics of the Baseball Swing, that seed of curiosity germinated and led me to Colorado, where I attended a Hitting Certification in 2012. The desire for more hasn't stopped since. From Pitch-A-Palooza to ABCA, SlugFest to NFCA to On BaseU and beyond, there has always been a hunger to figure this thing out, with the intent of helping my son become the best version of himself.

Here's what all those educational venues did: They equipped me with a better understanding of the hardware. Here's what they didn't do. What they didn't do was teach me how to install the software. Because even the best clinics and certifications focused almost exclusively on mechanics. Positions. Patterns. Movement. The musculoskeletal system. Everything from the neck down.

I became a hardware specialist. I didn't even know the operating system existed.

WHAT IS THE HARDWARE?

Hardware is the part of hitting most people recognize. It's what you can film, measure, slow down, compare, analyze. Think of the swing as the engine, the transmission, the chassis. It's physical. Blueprint. The foundation, walls, and roof of your hitting house.

The swing is energy transfer, ground to legs to hips to torso to hands to barrel to ball. It's Load (stabilizing power), Stride (positioning power), Rotation (releasing power), and Contact (delivering power).

Hardware includes:

- Mechanics
- Sequencing
- Strength & power
- Bat speed

- Rhythm & movement patterns
- Swing paths
- Timing patterns
- The athletic "engine" behind execution

The brain governs all of this. It's your operating system for movement. When you train mechanics or movement quality, the brain is storing those patterns so they can be recalled instantly, without conscious thought.

All important. All necessary. But all incomplete.

In short: the swing is the hardware, the physical transfer of energy from the ground up through the body into the bat to hit the ball.

Google "essential elements of hitting." You'll see the usual list: proper stance and balance, a powerful load, efficient timing, advanced hand-eye coordination, quiet focused head, effective hip rotation, quick and direct hand path, strength and bat speed, ground force production, and sequencing all rotational segments.

This is the typical hardware checklist discussed throughout social media, in most cages, and at most practices. Listen, all of these are important to becoming the best version of yourself. But if you are limited to just this list, I will make the case that you will never meet that version of yourself.

Why? Because this list is only the hardware.

Hardware is essential. But here's the truth: Hardware alone cannot solve a software problem. And most slumps, failures, inconsistencies, and confidence issues are software issues, not hardware ones.

Here's what you need to understand: The closer you get to the college and professional levels, the less you hear great hitting coaches talking about these mechanical elements during the season. Why? Because they're focused on software, approach, timing, pitch selection, and game planning. They're teaching hitting, not just upgrading the swing.

It took me way too long to understand that distinction. A high school softball player taught me this.

WHAT IS THE SOFTWARE?

If hardware is the body and the brain, software is the mind.

Software is how you think, how you process, how you choose, how you plan, how you see the game. It includes:

- Approach
- Plan
- Pitch selection
- Understanding of your identity as a hitter
- Decision-making speed
- Recognition patterns
- Discipline
- Confidence
- Intent

> Hardware is what swings the bat. Software determines when, why, and at what time you swing the bat.

This difference is everything.

A great swing doesn't matter if it's pointed at the wrong pitch. A powerful body doesn't matter if the mind is indecisive. Clean mechanics don't matter if the hitter guesses wrong.

Software determines outcomes long before the hardware ever moves.

LP'S LESSON: WHEN SOFTWARE SAVED THE SEASON

Seeing Clearly Through the Hardware Lens

It was 2017. I was watching a local softball game featuring one of the best hitters in the state at the time. Standing alongside some "dad experts," I made an observation: "LP has so much potential," I said aloud. The looks I received from the dads expressed what they were thinking: How could you say such a thing about the best hitter that has ever played at this school, one of the best ever in the county or state?

What they didn't see was her intent to pull her hands in to stay "inside" the ball, resulting in eliminating the whipping of the barrel and creating a power reduction on the inner part of the plate. I'm not ashamed to tell people that God has given me the gift of slow-motion assessment for a real-time swing. I could clearly tell how she'd been instructed and what opportunities and vulnerabilities she would face. If I had the opportunity to call pitches against her, I knew exactly where to attack to keep her from doing damage.

Oftentimes, we describe players as big fish in a small pond, without realizing it. The problem? A lot of fishermen (gurus) never test their own skills in the deep sea. Or, when their fish make it to deeper waters, they don't survive.

The First Encounter

Later that summer, while serving as a second set of eyes for a local travel ball organization, who did I see? LP.

"You're LP," I said.

"Yes sir," she responded.

"You've been taught to drive the knob to the ball, haven't you?"

I wish I had a photo of the look on her face. Her expression said everything: How does this stranger know what I've been doing to develop my swing? Her face changed. Not confusion, recognition. Like I'd just described a recurring dream she'd never told anyone about.

"How do you…" She stopped herself. "Yeah."

I then shared with her what pitches she did not hit the hardest. Now her eyes narrowed. Not defensive. Curious.

The Cage Visit That Changed Everything

Weeks later, after arriving at a summer tournament, LP approached me as I was walking towards the fields with a look of great urgency.

"We need to go to the cage. My swing sucks," she said in frustration.

"Wait, you play in a couple hours," I said. I didn't have the confidence or belief to provide her a quick mechanical fix, because I knew it takes time to make physical adjustments, and a bucket of balls isn't enough time. Worst of all, I would make her think. I know a thinking hitter leads to an inconsistent swing, and I didn't want her to get any worse.

Let's just say she encouraged me to see what I could see. So off to the cage we went.

Following a few flips, I noticed something immediately, even though it wasn't what I'd been trained to look for.

"LP, there is nothing wrong with your swing. You're getting your foot down too soon."

That's it. One sentence. Not about her hardware. About her software, her timing, her internal clock, her decision speed. This was the very reason she was rolling over outside pitches to the left side of the field. This was a software issue, not a hardware one!

Most people think their hardware breaks down under pressure. In reality, their software collapses first. The body looks bad because the mind made a poor decision. LP's hardware was fine. Her software just needed a quick recalibration.

HONESTY MOMENT

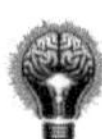 When was the last time you had a conversation with your player about pitch selection that lasted longer than 5 minutes? Followed with application in the cage?

The Result

A couple hours later, following LP's first at-bat, she produced a hard ground ball to the second baseman. I immediately walked to the dugout and told her, "Stay right there, don't change anything!"

The very next at-bat: double off the wall.

One adjustment. Not hardware, software. I didn't change how she swung. I changed when she committed.

You'd think that would have changed everything about how I coached, right?

It didn't.

I'd Been Upgrading Hardware, and Still Didn't Change

My very next hitting session after LP's breakthrough, I walked into the cage with another student like nothing had happened. I set up the tee. I grabbed the video camera. I started doing exactly what I'd always done: analyzing foot placement, checking rotation, correcting back arm position, obsessing over bat path. Foot down. Rotation. Back arm. Back leg. The same old hardware stuff.

What was I doing?

I was being blinded by my hardware biases and beliefs! More on this in chapter 10. Two days ago, LP was struggling. I didn't upgrade her hardware. I updated her software with one sentence, and she went from frustrated to double-off-the-wall in two at-bats. I didn't touch her mechanics. I addressed her mind.

But here I was, back to teaching mechanical adjustments like it never happened.

A hardware specialist teaches positions and patterns. A hitting coach installs software and upgrades decisions. One focuses on how you move your body. The other focuses on how to think and make decisions.

I'd spent years becoming an expert in hardware, attending certifications, studying biomechanics, analyzing kinematic sequences, understanding stretch-shortening cycles, tracking ball exit speed and bat speed and vertical bat angles and angular velocity. The hardware was what I studied, what I taught and what my players became. My bias, their beliefs, became performance barriers that I have to own up to.

What's sad, this LP experience came after I read The Science of Hitting! This is an example of how your environment can direct your attention to something specific, causing you not to see what is in plain sight!

THE CONVERSATION THAT BEAT A THOUSAND DRILLS

"I Went 0-3 Looking for a Curve"

The real transformation happened with LP the following spring. LP came to me after a game.

"I went 0-3," she said.

"What were you looking for?" I asked.

"I was looking for a curve, the only problem, I kept swinging at the screw, only because it was a strike."

I thought, "Oh my, that's it!"

I looked at her and said something that would become the foundation of everything I teach: "You never swing at what you aren't looking for with less than two strikes." I proceeded to tell LP that when you have less than two strikes, if her body committed to a pitch her mind hadn't decided on, miss on purpose.

This is software installation. Pure and simple. This is teaching the mind to override the body when necessary. This is understanding that in-season hitting is not thinking. It's choosing.

The mind should only be responsible for choosing whether the pitch matches your plan, speed and location, and staying committed to the decision. Everything else must run automatically.

The Breakthrough

The following week, I stood next to those same dads, the ones who thought LP was already perfect, with my camera rolling. LP stepped into the box with less than two strikes. The pitch came: inside, technically a strike. Her body started to commit, weight shifted, hands moved, but meanwhile something stopped her. She swung and missed. On purpose!

"YES!" I shouted, startling everyone around me. "She did it!"

One of the dads turned to me, confused. "What was that? She had just swung and missed!" With less than two strikes.

I kept my mouth shut. How could I explain that what looked like failure was actually a breakthrough? Her hardware had started to commit, but her software had overridden it. So she followed my instruction: miss on purpose.

She was learning to separate instinct from intention. To let her mind lead, not her reflexes. She was learning that during competition, the mind shifts:

From thinking → to deciding. From analyzing → to choosing. From "How do I hit?" → to "Is this my pitch?"

The dads thought her hardware broke down. I knew her software had just leveled up. This discipline was demonstrated, just as directed.

The Most Important Detail

Here's what makes LP's transformation so significant: She never had a lesson with me. Not one. No tee work. No drill sequences. No video analysis. No discussions about kinematic sequences or stretch-shortening cycles or launch angles. No mechanical adjustments. No hardware upgrades.

> She had one conversation about timing and one conversation about decision-making. That's it. Software installation. She went on to become the #3 home run hitter in the nation at the DII JUCO level her freshman season with a .429 batting average.

The most impactful instruction I ever gave didn't involve upgrading hardware. It involved installing better software.

That's when I learned: Sometimes the fastest way to improve isn't through more information, it's through clarity. Not more drills, but better decisions. Not mechanical perfection, but mental preparation.

When fancy drills are thrown around and your timeline is full of "the best drill today," we become biased to the current thing and not the customer's thing. We're playing Russian roulette with tomorrow's performance. "I could not change my training because I would not change my thinking."

LP taught me that hitting is a conversation, not a to-do list.

HONESTY MOMENT

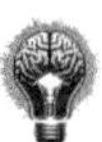 Close the book for 30 seconds. Think about your last practice. When you struggled, what did you fix first? Your hardware or your software?

WHEN SOFTWARE UPGRADES HARDWARE

Here's the beauty of training the mind: Every software improvement upgrades hardware execution.

A clearer plan cleans up movement. Better pitch selection sharpens mechanics. Better timing decisions increase power. Better rhythm awareness improves adjustability. Better identity creates better intent.

When software improves, hardware has fewer problems to solve. You swing at better pitches. You start sooner. Your body organizes better. Your timing stabilizes. Your movements simplify.

LP's success should have been an isolated case, the exception that proved the rule. Except it wasn't isolated. The more I paid attention, the more I saw the pattern: Players with the prettiest hardware often had the worst software.

How often have you witnessed this? The player who looks flawless in the cage but struggles in games. The player who was one of the best in the state in high school but has a tough time adjusting once they arrive at the college level. Why aren't those efficient swings making a smooth transition to college competition?

The Inundation Problem

The problem is the inundation of hardware information, combined with the belief that hardware upgrades are the only requirements for consistency at the plate. Yes, very talented players may have the God-given ability to coordinate their hands and eyes with a knack for getting the barrel to the ball. But catch this: relying on your talent can come with great risk as you move up from high school or travel ball to college.

Consider this: There are eleven systems that make up the human body. As each system develops prior to birth, the last to be developed are the extremities (arms and legs). The first system to be developed is the central nervous system (brain and spinal cord). For whatever reason, when it comes to hitting instruction, that development is reversed. We start with the extremities, the arms, the legs, the body parts, and ignore the central nervous system.

Oftentimes we upgrade hardware from the outside in, when we should be installing software from the inside out.

Even when considering the extremities, they are not the same for all players.

The Variety Problem

Once these systems create a complete human being and future hitter, consider the following ranges:

Gender (Male and female)

Height (5'3" to 6'7")

Weight (110 lbs to 250 lbs)

Arm lengths (Vary significantly)

Body types (Loose movers and tight movers)

Muscle fibers (Fast-twitch and slow-twitch)

Visual Learners, Kinesthetic Learners, and Auditory Learners.

All of these influence how the body produces rotational movement patterns. Teaching a consistent movement pattern can be such a challenge for any instructor or coach with a variety of sizes, movement types and learning styles. Would you use a sports car the same way you use a half-ton pickup truck? Why would you have a 5'3", 112-pound female who's a loose mover try to make the same move as a 6' 3", 215-pound male who's a tight mover?

If I'm a coach with 20 hitters on the team, I can bucket them all into one hardware configuration. Here's the question, at what cost? Are we sacrificing what will allow them to be the most competitive version of themselves?

The Comfort vs. Competition Problem

Often, the pretty hardware has an ugly outcome for some pitch speeds, locations, and shapes. Consider this: When a player spends the majority of their time on the tee with a fixed position, what are you really preparing for? Or, more importantly, what are you NOT going to be preparing for? The pitcher 43 or 60 feet away is not grooving a single pitch to match your grooved hardware.

When it comes down to it, I question the influence comfort has on player development. Most of us will agree that a swing looks great in the cage. However, after a few at-bats, how does what look so eloquent in a controlled environment look so chaotic in a competitive environment?

Unfortunately, when pretty doesn't produce for those who have worked most of their adolescent lives to become the best they can be, they realize too late: the time, money, and beliefs were all centered around a biased hardware specialization that no longer works when the competition gets better. Do you know a player who hit .350+ in high school but less than .200 in college?

Here's the truth that will make you uncomfortable: They were always a .200 hitter. Their .350 average in high school was built on three things: Inferior pitching that couldn't exploit their holes, cage-confidence that created the illusion of ability, and God-given talent that masked their lack of approach.

On the other hand, when college pitchers match your talent, they will find your weaknesses and throw three speeds to six spots. That's when you will discover your talent and pretty hardware isn't enough. The pretty swing wasn't enough. You had the hardware. You never installed the software.

COMMON SENSE NOT COMMONLY SEEN: THE ALANA JOHNSON PRINCIPLE

My First Real Hitting Lesson

 If pitching is intended to disrupt the rhythm and timing of the hitter (and I doubt you'll disagree) then hitting must be about staying in rhythm and being on time.

HONESTY MOMENT

Has everything I've ever heard about hitting been talking or teaching?

The Day Everything Changed

January 8, 2019. Alana Johnson walked into my cage for the first time. I was a little nervous. She was a future Power 5 player, the kind of talent that doesn't come through your doors often. The kind of talent where one wrong piece of advice could derail a career.

The pressure was immediate: Don't mess this up. Everyone's counting on you not to mess this God-given talent up.

Every instinct I'd developed over years of coaching screamed at me to do what I'd always done: pull out the camera, analyze her swing, find something to fix, prove my value. Then I remembered LP. I remembered that the most productive thing I'd ever done for a hitter was to NOT upgrade her hardware.

So, before Alana took a single swing, I said something that went against everything I'd been trained to do: "You will play at the next level. Now, if you want to be GREAT at the next level, you must understand that not all strikes are made equal."

I understood that hitting is much like operating a vehicle:

The swing = The vehicle (car/Ferrari/machine)

Hitting = The driver/navigation/knowing where to go

Hardware = The engine

Software = The GPS/map/driver training

Practice = The test track

Games = Real roads with traffic.

Lana knew how to operate her engine; she just needed to learn how to read a road map. Alana looked at me, and we went to work. We minored in hardware tweaking but majored in software installation. She was already one of the most productive hitters I'd ever witnessed. Her hardware worked. No need to change who she was as a mover.

This was the day I started using common sense not commonly seen: If it's working, don't fix it. Enhance the mind and body, don't rebuild it. What Alana needed wasn't hardware adjustment, it was software installation. She needed to understand the timing of the strike zone and the positions of the strike zone. To hunt the pitches that were expected. To maximize her natural strengths instead of trying to be perfect everywhere.

The simplicity of Alana's development, and her father Chad's buy-in was centered around core principles of hitting, not around perfecting positions I thought she should be in. That's when everything clicked for me. The principles of hitting that are essential for Lana, even if her hardware left her. You can hit good pitching without your best swing. You cannot hit good pitching without your software.

THE .426 HITTER WITH THREE HOME RUNS: WHEN OFFSEASON SOFTWARE CHANGES EVERYTHING

Madison Moak was one of Alana's teammates, one of the most versatile players I've ever seen. She could do everything: Hit for power, Push bunt, Drag bunt, and Slap hit. The few times I had the opportunity to call pitches against her, I never got her out. This was Power 5 talent, no question. Her talent could have allowed her to play anywhere in the country. She chose to stay closer to home.

THE CAGE VISIT

In the winter of her sophomore year, Madison walked into my cage. Less than 2½ months before the season. I asked her the question I ask everyone: "How many home runs did you have last year?"

"Three," she said.

I paused, in shock. Knowing what type of athlete she is! Her home run numbers should be higher than that!

Madison added, "I batted .426. Sixty-three hits. Twenty-nine RBIs."

THE PROBLEM

Let me paint the picture for you: A Power 5-caliber hitter. Versatile. Athletic. Talented enough that the average coach and the average pitcher had zero shot against her. But she had three home runs. Three. Not because she couldn't hit for power. She absolutely could. Something was missing.

Her hardware was elite, but software had never been upgraded.

THE CONVERSATION

Me: "Let me ask you something," I said. "Do you have an approach?"

Madison: Silence.

Me: "What's your rhythm like in the box?"

Madison: More silence.

Me: "What pitches are you hunting?"

She looked at me like I was speaking a different language.

THE PLAN: OFFSEASON SOFTWARE INSTALLATION

We only made one minor adjustment to her hardware. A better body position to produce a better path. We focused on installing software, the kind of software that could only be built in the offseason.

This is where thinking belongs. This is where curiosity belongs. This is where deep understanding is built.

Offseason is the time to install:

- Approach principles
- Recognition patterns
- Decision-making logic
- Understanding of speed and location
- Your identity as a hitter
- Your winning plan

It's also where you test. Where you question. Where you break things down and rebuild them stronger.

This is where the mind is active learning, evaluating, analyzing.

For Madison, we focused on three things:

TIMING (When do you stop? When do you commit?)

RHYTHM (How do you adapt to slower?)

DISCIPLINE (What pitches do you crush? What pitches do you struggle with? What will you hunt with less than two strikes?)

That's it. Rhythm and discipline. Software installation. The 90%, not the 10%.

We spent a couple of sessions before the season building her software so that when the season arrived, her mind could shift from thinking to deciding. From analyzing to choosing. From "How do I hit?" to "Is this my pitch?"

THE RESULT

A few months later, Madison finished her sophomore season: .503 batting average, 16 home runs, 69 RBIs, and 94 hits.

.426 with 3 home runs to .503 with 16 home runs. We never rebuilt her hardware. We just installed the software. We just taught her how to hunt instead of reacting. We just gave her rhythm awareness. We just added discipline to her approach.

THE LESSON

Table 1.0 - Madison Moak's Year-to-Year Transformation

Category	Freshman Year	Sophomore Year	Improvement
Batting Average	.426	.503	+.077
Home Runs	3	16	+13
RBIs	29	69	+40
Hits	63	94	+31

Madison's story proves what this entire book is about: You can have elite hardware and still leave production on the table if you don't install the software. She had the Damage. She always had the Damage. She just needed Decision and Discipline.

Most players only train the hardware. Madison learned to train both. 13 additional home runs later, she understood something most players never discover: You cannot think your way to better mechanics. You cannot swing your way to better decisions.

The best hitters see the connection: The mind directs. The body executes. The software instructs. The hardware performs. The choice comes first. The movement follows.

Talent gets you noticed. Approach gets you paid.

THE EIGHT CORE PRINCIPLES OF HITTING (THE SOFTWARE)

If hitting is about staying in rhythm and being on time, then these are the software principles that allow you to do that:

CORE PRINCIPLE #1: Know Your Strengths

What it means: Identify the specific speeds and locations where you consistently hit the ball hard.

Why it matters: Knowing your strengths maximizes confidence when facing a pitcher where you maintain your rhythm and he/she throws to a position that pairs with your intended barrel path. Pitches and speeds in your hot zone, your confidence soars, you see the ball better, your timing improves.

The trap to avoid: Thinking you should be able to do damage to every pitch and location with the same path and timing. You can't. Neither can anyone else. Stop trying. You can crush some pitches. Others eat you alive. This isn't a weakness. This is reality. Even Mike Trout has holes. The difference? He knows exactly where his holes are. You probably don't.

The test: Can you draw your hot zones and cold zones on a strike zone chart right now? If not, you're guessing. Guessing makes you prey.

The truth: When you know your holes, you can protect them. When you know your strengths, you can hunt them.

CORE PRINCIPLE #2: Know Your Weaknesses

What it means: Identify what speeds and locations you don't hit well. Be honest about your holes.

Why it matters: Knowing your weakness should accomplish several things. First, it could increase your hunger to decrease the hole in your swing through compensations or adjustments. Second, without those compensations or corrective movements, you should maximize your discipline for the vulnerable area or speed until two strikes. Better pitchers will attack your weaknesses. If you don't know what they are, you can't defend them. You can either work to fix them or avoid them until you have to swing.

The trap to avoid: Pretending you don't have weaknesses. Every hitter has holes. The question is whether you'll acknowledge them and address them or ignore them and let pitchers exploit them. Not knowing your weakness and swinging at them is like fishing in a large lake with two fish, wishing for a bite.

CORE PRINCIPLE #3: Ability to Time

What it means: Know how YOU time. Are you timing off the pitcher's release or off the ball? How do you time your load, forward move, foot-down decision, and decision to rotate?

Why it matters: Once you identify how you time, then you can hunt speed or a side of the plate. If you don't understand your timing mechanism, you're guessing. Against good pitching, guessing gets you out. Have timing awareness. Some hitters start their movement off the pitcher's first move. Others wait to see the ball out of the hand. There's no single right way, but you must know YOUR way.

The trap to avoid: Never thinking about how you time. Most hitters have no idea whether they time off the pitcher or the ball. They just "see it and hit it", which works until it doesn't.

Quick exercise: Next time you're in the cage, try timing off the pitcher's release. Then try timing off the ball flight. Which feels more natural? That's your timing mechanism. Now you have data instead of hope.

CORE PRINCIPLE #4: Game Planning Strategies

What it means: The ability to take pitcher information or make location-speed decisions and properly simulate your at-bat-to-at-bat approach. Game planning with or without pitcher information.

Why it matters: When you have information about a pitcher's tendencies, sequences, and out-pitches, you can anticipate. When you can anticipate, you can hunt. When you hunt, you hit. The best hitters game plan like chess players, working three to four days ahead on what they know the pitcher will throw. Not Russian roulette, hoping the pitch will land into the barrel.

The trap to avoid: Walking into the box with no plan. "I'll just see what they throw" is not a strategy, it's hope. Hope is not an approach. Walking to the plate without a plan is like taking a test you didn't study for. You might get lucky. Luck isn't a strategy. Honestly, your talent may allow you to get away without game planning. However, when you meet the equivalent talent in the circle or mound, with the pitching coach's assistance, then what?

Note: Game planning does not require pitcher information in advance. More on this later.

CORE PRINCIPLE #5: Application of Discipline

What it means: Realizing that all strikes are not made equal. Sticking to your approach even when it's uncomfortable.

Why it matters: Even during a hitter's positive count, you have options. You had a plan to be early for the screw or fastball in, and you started late? If it's not a hit-and-run, this could be a great opportunity to take the pitch and reset. Discipline is what separates professional hitters from amateurs. It's the willingness to take a strike in your weak zone to get a pitch in your strong zone.

The trap to avoid: "That was a strike, I should have swung." No. That was a strike in your hole. You made the right decision.

THE PROBLEM: We treat every soft contact like a hardware failure.

THE TRUTH: Most are software failures, not hardware failures.

CORE PRINCIPLE #6: Identifying Adaptation Abilities (Two-Strike Approach)

What it means: Your two-strike approach and production. Can you adapt when you're forced to expand or protect?

Why it matters: You won't always get your pitch with less than two strikes. The best hitters can adjust their approach with two strikes, expanding their zone slightly, shortening their swing, or hunting different locations. Can you cover up-and-in at 65 mph, down at 58 mph, and middle at 50 mph? Of course you can, with the right adjustment tool in your toolbox. The key here is the right timing, tempo, and path (TTP).

The trap to avoid: Approaching every count the same way. Zero strikes and two strikes require different mentalities, different zones, different discipline. Two strikes. Your swing must cover 0-2 strikes, breaking balls outside AND fastballs in. Can you do both? Or are you just hoping?

CORE PRINCIPLE #7: Developing Compensations

What it means: When the swing breaks or feel leaves, do you have answers? Compensations are essential when you can't get your body to position the barrel in a spot with the most efficient natural movement.

Why it matters: Do you have answers to cheat to the spot you know the pitch is coming to, yet it's your most vulnerable when moving naturally? Can you adjust mid-at-bat, mid-game, mid-season? What is your go-to when your body can't produce its 100% swing? The best hitters have a toolbox of compensations. They can cheat to speed, cheat to location, or adjust their path when their A-swing isn't working.

The trap to avoid: Only having one way to swing. When that breaks, you're done. Your A-swing breaks mid-game. Now what? If your only answer is "keep swinging and hope," you're not a predator. You're the prey.

CORE PRINCIPLE #8: Identifying Your Misses

What it means: Can you identify your miss? Was your primary miss over, under, early, late, or across? Are you able to take this information following a pitch or at-bat and pair it up with a corrective movement or compensation?

Why it matters: Self-correction is the highest form of hitting IQ. If you can diagnose your miss in real-time, you can adjust pitch-to-pitch. If you can't, you'll make the same mistake three times before someone tells you what's wrong.

The trap to avoid: Blaming your hardware all the time. "I just missed it" isn't analysis. "I was under it because I was late" is an analysis. One leads to adjustment. The other leads to frustration.

Your last strikeout: Don't know why you struck out? Then you can't fix it. You'll do it again next at-bat.

Why These Principles Matter More Than You Think

The discussion of these principles is often described as being "too much" for players. I would agree, whenever the individual is limited to awareness without application. Your best hitting coaches should scout their own hitters just as much as they scout the pitchers. This is called understanding your own, which can then position you to maximize and customize the simplicity of each player's needs.

Why don't we hear much about these principles? I'll provide my perspective on that, although I prefer not to speculate on why others don't teach them. What I know is this: When you collaborate with an elite athlete's hardware with proper software installation, you have the potential to expose pitchers in a way that would be unfair to them.

HONESTY MOMENT

Real talk: How many of these eight principles have you actually learned (player), or are teaching (instructor/coach). Actually, taught with the same intensity you teach stride length, rotation, or your favorite drill?

Count them. That number tells you something.

THE TRUTH ABOUT ELITE HITTERS

Watch the best hitters in the world and you'll see two truths:

Their hardware is elite. Movement quality, rhythm, timing, intent, top tier.

Their software is even better. Elite hitters don't make elite decisions by accident.

They know:

What pitch they're hunting

Why they're hunting it

When in the count they're shifting gears

Which speeds or locations carry danger

How their timing needs to adjust

What the pitcher is trying to disrupt

They're not smarter than everyone else. They're simply running better software and they trained it.

WHEN SOFTWARE IS ACTIVE AND WHEN IT MUST STAY QUIET

The mind is powerful, when used at the right time. Hitters fail when they don't understand the two modes:

1. OFFSEASON: SOFTWARE ON

This is where thinking belongs. This is where curiosity belongs. This is where deep understanding is built. Offseason is the time to install approach principles, recognition patterns, decision-making logic, understanding of speed and location, your identity as a hitter, and your winning plan.

It's also where you test. Where you question. Where you break things down and rebuild them stronger. This is where the mind is active learning, evaluating, and analyzing.

2. IN-SEASON: SOFTWARE SIMPLIFIED

During the season, the mind shifts:

From thinking → to deciding. From analyzing → to choosing. From "How do I hit?" → to "Is this my pitch?"

In competition, too much software activity crashes the system.

The mind should only be responsible for:

Choosing whether the pitch matches your plan (speed + location)

Staying committed to the decision

Staying composed under pressure

Everything else is hardware. Everything else must run automatically.

This is the separation: In-season hitting is not thinking. It's choosing.

YOUR RESPONSIBILITY AS A HITTER

If you want to hit at a high level consistently, repeatedly and predictably you cannot choose between software and hardware.

You must train both. You must understand both. You must know when each serves you... and when each gets in your way.

You cannot think your way to better mechanics. You cannot swing your way to better decisions.

The best hitters see the connection: The mind directs. The body executes. The software instructs. The hardware performs. The choice comes first. The movement follows.

When you combine elite hardware with proper software installation, you create something that feels unfair to pitchers. Most hitters show up with just the hardware or just natural software. Rarely are both intentionally trained.

The hardware gives you the ability to do damage when you get your pitch. The software gives you the discipline to wait for that pitch. Together, they're devastating.

Here's what you need to understand: You can't teach hitting by only upgrading hardware. Ted Williams was right 55 years ago with the 50%. In most cases hitting is up to 90% from the neck up, 90% software. Yet we're still spending 90%-100% of our time from the neck down, obsessing over positions, angles, and movements while ignoring the decisions, timing, and discipline that determine success.

LP taught me that one software installation is worth more than a hundred reps with perfect hardware. Alana taught me that knowing when NOT to fix hardware is as important as knowing how to fix it. Madison taught me that proper offseason software installation transforms good hitters into elite ones.

All three taught me that the best hitters aren't the ones with the prettiest hardware, they're the ones who understand what to swing at, when to commit, and how to hunt their strengths while minimizing their weaknesses.

So here's the question that should keep you up tonight: Are you upgrading your players' hardware? Or are you installing their software?

There's a difference. A massive, career-defining difference. It's the gap between cage stars and game producers. Between high school success and college survival. Between mechanical perfection and competitive dominance.

All strikes are not made equal and knowing which ones to hunt changes everything.

You now understand the difference between hardware and software. Between swing specialists and hitting coaches. Between teaching positions and teaching decisions. Now here's the problem: even if you understand this distinction intellectually, you're probably still training like you don't.

Right now, somewhere in America, a talented player is in a batting cage taking their 87th swing down the middle at the same speed. They feel great. They look great. Everyone's impressed. Their hardware looks perfect.

But their software is running on fumes. And they're preparing for absolutely nothing.

This book is about installing the software your season will depend on. By the time you finish it, your hardware will be allowed to do what it was trained to do, without interference, confusion, panic, or hesitation.

And that's when the game slows down. That's when confidence rises. That's when your swing finally plays the way it was built. That's when you start hitting from the neck up.

In the next chapter, you're going to discover why everything you think is "working" in the cage is working against you in games. Why cage bombs create false confidence. Why feel-good training leads to game-day failure. And why the players who look the best in practice often perform the worst under pressure.

The truth about cage training is going to make you angry. Especially if you've been doing it wrong for years.

Anger leads to change. Change leads to breakthroughs.

Are you ready to destroy everything you thought you knew about practice?

Table 1.1 - The Eight Core Principles of Hitting

Principle	What It Means	Why It Matters	The Trap to Avoid
Know Your Strengths	Identify speeds/locations where you consistently hit hard	Maximizes confidence when hunting pitches	Thinking you can damage every pitch equally
Know Your Weaknesses	Identify what speeds/locations you don't hit well	Allows you to protect or avoid vulnerable areas	Pretending you don't have holes
Ability to Time	Recognize when your load, stride, and launch connect	Separates hitters who react from hitters who plan	Mistaking rhythm for timing
Game Planning Strategies	Creating plans for pitcher types and sequences	Gives structure to your at-bats	Relying on memory instead of preparation
Application of Discipline	Swinging with clear intention	Reinforces approach consistency	Over-swinging at marginal pitches
Two-Strike Approach	Adjusting without panic	Increases in-zone contact rate	Overcompensating and losing aggression
Developing Compensations	Using body adjustments when time is short	Keeps you competitive vs. elite pitching	Relying on compensations instead of corrections
Identifying Your Misses	Understanding your contact tendencies	Turns failure into feedback	Blaming mechanics instead of awareness

CHAPTER 2

CAGE BOMBS AND HARD TRUTHS

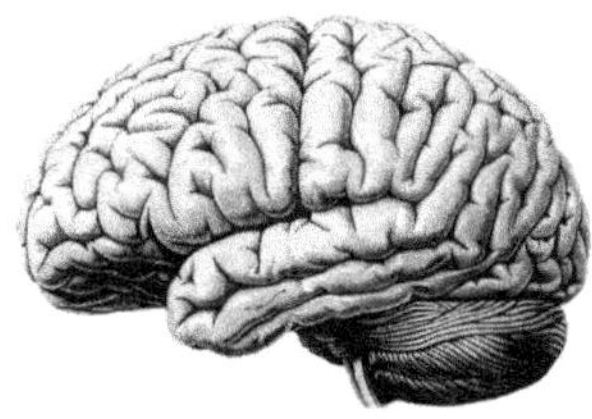

What 10-Year-Olds and Softball Players Taught Me About Real Hitting Development

"Five pitches with consequences will develop a hitter faster than fifty-five pitches with none. You know this. You're just afraid to implement it." - Coaching wisdom

THE PROBLEM

Thursday evening, your cage is alive with the sound of success: crack, crack, crack. Your 14-year-old bombs twenty straight pitches, barrels blazing, balls rocketing off the back net. Dad's filming. Mom's smiling. You're nodding. Everyone leaves feeling great. You think you just received a killer lesson.

Saturday morning, first at-bat: strikeout looking at a changeup. Second at-bat: weak pop up on a rise ball you never saw in the cage. Third at-bat: ground ball on a curve. Final line: 0-for-4. Weekend wraps: 2-for-16. One hit came against a team that won't sniff college ball. The other hit. Was it really an earned hit?

THE TRUTH

Monday morning, mom or dad sends the text: "I don't understand. She crushed it in her lesson Thursday. What happened?" Here's what happened: Her swing is fine. It's always been fine. You know that lesson you just charged $75-$125 for? That wasn't a lesson. That was batting practice. They threw her 120 pitches at one speed to one location, and she demolished them. It felt great. It looked great. It prepared her for nothing.

Saturday's pitcher threw her three different speeds to 6 different locations, and she had no idea what to swing at or when to commit. She was trained to swing. She never trained to hit.

STOP AND THINK

How many players look better in the cage than they do in games? If the answer is "most of them" or "all of them," keep reading. You're about to discover why, and it's not your players' fault. It may just be the training environment.

THE CAGE BOMB ILLUSION

THE PROBLEM: You are convinced that volume equals development. That 100 swings are better than 10. That happy players mean effective lessons.

THE TRUTH: Cage bombs feel like progress. They look like success. They produce nothing when speed changes, location moves, and consequences arrive.

THE MASSAGE METAPHOR

During my travel ball coaching days, you hear this from parents constantly: "He/she hit the ball so well in his lesson the other day. I don't know why he's having so much trouble this weekend." That parent just paid you to fill a knowledge void. What you gave them was feel-good batting practice. Comfort.

Think about this: When you go for a massage, there's the rubdown and there's the deep tissue. The rubdown? Heaven. You're relaxed. You're loose. You float out of there feeling incredible. But your shoulder still has that knot. Your back still has that tension. The rubdown felt amazing. It fixed nothing. That's your cage.

You're giving rubdowns when your players need deep tissue work. The tournament pitcher? She's the deep tissue therapist who's about to expose every weakness you chose to massage away instead of address. Cage bombs are the rubdown. They feel good. They look good. Everyone leaves happy. They don't fix anything. They never have.

THE PIANO RECITAL METAPHOR

Your player practices 'Twinkle Twinkle Little Star' for six months, same tempo, same key, same everything. Perfect practice. Recital day comes. The piano is out of tune. The room has different acoustics. They're nervous. They freeze. That's the cage bomb trap. Perfect practice in controlled conditions. Zero adaptation when variables change.

WHY CAGE BOMBS EXIST

Let's be honest about why you're running feel-good lessons.

REASON #1: CLIENT RETENTION - THE PROBLEM: Some instructors are running a restaurant. Table 12 wants dessert for dinner, no vegetables, no protein, just chocolate cake and ice cream. You know it's not what they need. However, they're paying. So, you give them cake and ice cream. THE TRUTH: That's cage bombs. Sweet. Satisfying. Slowly destroying your players' development while padding your bank account. You're afraid to lose a client.

REASON #2: "THE PLAYER ISN'T READY YET" - THE GPS METAPHOR: Some teach hitting like a GPS giving directions to someone walking versus someone driving. They can't tell a ten-year-old to "feel the ground forces transfer through the kinetic chain" any more than you can tell a pedestrian to "take Exit 47 in 3 miles." THE TRUTH: The ten-year-old doesn't need to wait until they're twenty to understand damage zones. Age-appropriate instruction means translated information.

REASON #3: LIMITED INFORMATION - THE PROBLEM: The instruction is limited to the information you possess. THE TRUTH: This reason is the most forgivable, and the most fixable. Limited information is just a gap. Gaps can be filled.

CRITICAL QUESTION: Which reason are they hiding behind? Client retention? "They're not ready yet"? Limited information? Circle one. Now ask yourself: What would happen if they stopped hiding behind it this week?

MY EDUCATION BY 10-YEAR-OLDS

The Setup

I was about to become the best 10u hitting coach in Mississippi. At least, that's what I thought. After my son RJ transitioned to school baseball, I was asked to assist with a 10u baseball team. This shouldn't be a problem, right? I was a gifted communicator with experience coaching teenage youth. I was sure the parents would buy in and take my lead. Who else was putting themselves in a position to ensure these young men would become some of the best baseball players in Mississippi?

I was convinced I'd create the best 10u hitters in Mississippi. Two weeks later, I'd created nothing. Same swings. Same results. Same problems. The only thing that changed was my pride; it was demolished. That demolition was the best thing that could have happened. Those 10-year-olds taught me more about hitting instruction than a decade of clinics or conferences ever had.

The Reality Check

After two weeks and four sessions, I faced reality: these 10-year-olds looked the same. Worse, I looked exactly like every other instructor, throwing batting practice and calling it instruction. Something had to change. If I was going to develop some of the best hitters in the state, I needed to make an adjustment from the typical drill work. This wasn't working.

A great time to practice what we preach: "Make an adjustment." But here's what I learned: Coaches should make the first adjustment. We ask athletes to adjust all day long but how often do we adjust ourselves? How often do we look in the mirror and admit that our methods aren't working, no matter how much we know? Even though I had a lot of answers, I didn't have all the answers.

I decided to assess the players' strengths and build "hitting" practices around intent to do damage and discipline, two of the three pillars of hitting. This required some data collection, but no equipment we had to calibrate or connect to WiFi. Before you roll your eyes, this is where I decided to maximize simplicity by using "simple" data: PPA. Pen, Paper, and Arithmetic were the tools of simplicity.

THE PPA METHOD: SIMPLICITY OVER TECHNOLOGY

The Assessment Was Embarrassingly Simple

Here's what I did: 20 pitches per player (10 up in the zone, 10 down in the zone), mark each result: weak contact, hard contact on a line, or miss, count where they did damage most consistently, and that became their damage zone. No technology. No launch monitors. No $5,000 equipment. No WiFi. Just honest observation of where each player naturally did damage. That's it. That's the whole assessment. But it changed everything.

Let me show you what changed:

BEFORE THE PPA METHOD: 20-25 pitches per round, all grooved to the same location; Players swinging at everything; "Great job!" after every contact, regardless of quality; Zero consequences for undisciplined swings; Parents happy, players confident, games disappointing.

AFTER THE PPA METHOD: 5 pitches per round, varied locations; Players hunting their damage zone only; Weak contact = round over; Immediate consequences for poor decisions; Parents confused, players focused, games transforming.

The change was shocking to everyone. Especially the parents.

FIVE PITCHES TO CHANGE EVERYTHING

The Revolutionary Decision

The next step was a shock for everyone but me. From that practice on, no player received more than 5 pitches in any round from me. This idea came from a breakfast conversation with Paul during my second Pitch-A-Palooza in 2017, where we discussed a simple question: Are we really teaching hitting?

When you throw 15-20 pitches per round and respond with "great job" to everything the player makes contact with, what are you teaching? Swinging? Or hitting? Can you imagine what was going through the minds of the parents and assistant coaches? My cage was for hitting. The other cages were for swinging. If they wanted more swings, they could get those outside of my cage or practice. We only had two practice days, an hour and a half each. One of those days was on the field. I didn't have time to teach a group of twelve 10-year-olds how to swing, yet I could teach them how to hit.

The Damage Zone Round

Each practice in my cage was a specific round, only five pitches. My favorite: the Damage Zone Round. Players could only swing at pitches in their damage zone with less than two strikes. Weak ground balls and pop-ups earned you an early exit from the cage or subtraction from remaining pitches.

When first implemented, a player said, "Coach, I didn't get enough swings." I responded:

> "I am not here to give you reps. I am here to teach you how to hit. This is not a rep cage."

To this day, the onlookers, parents watching from outside the fence, did not understand what was being developed in those young men.

Creating an environment that demanded decision, discipline and damage transitioned to the field was my intent.

JACK THE TEN-YEAR-OLD PITCHER WHO EXPOSED ME

When Good Systems Meet Real Competition

A few weeks after my players started developing better decision making and discipline, we ran into a problem I hadn't anticipated. We faced a young pitcher who did a phenomenal job of locating down and away, about a ball and a half off the plate. Of course, these were not strikes. The umpires were calling that location a strike, and my players were not prepared.

Pitch after pitch, my disciplined hitters took what should have been balls. Strike one. Strike two. Strike three. Without any offensive production, I knew I had to provide a simple adjustment. No problem, Mr. Coach has a solution.

The Solution That Failed

Prior to our next at-bat, I gathered all the players in a huddle, drew a line in the dirt about six inches outside the edge of home plate, and directed them: "Get on this line with your back foot. We're shifting the plate." Great idea, right? It didn't work. Not even a little bit. Players were confused. Their timing was off. Their positioning felt wrong. We looked like we'd never played baseball before.

But it wasn't their fault. This was not something we had practiced. I had taught them to recognize the zone, hunt their damage zone, apply discipline, and now, in the middle of a game with zero practice, I was asking them to do something completely different. I couldn't wait for that game to end. Frustrated. I knew exactly what I had to do. We were going back to practice, and we were going to fix this.

CREATING A "FIGURE IT OUT" ENVIRONMENT

The Sidewalk Chalk Solution

Prior to the next practice, I made a stop at Walmart to purchase sidewalk chalk. When the players arrived, they saw something new: a chalk line drawn on the ground, three balls off the plate, extending the strike zone dramatically.

I gathered them around. "Today, we're practicing for bad umpires. You see this chalk line? You must swing at anything between the chalk and the plate. Anything in that zone is a strike today." One player immediately raised his hand. "But coach, that's not a strike." "Neither were the strikes last Saturday," I responded. Everyone got quiet. They understood.

The First Pitch

First round. First player. My first pitch landed right between the plate and the chalk line, clearly outside, but inside our "bad umpire zone." The player took it. "You're out. Next player," I said. "But coach," the young man replied. "No buts. Follow instructions. That was a strike in Saturday's game, and you took it. So, you're out. Next."

It really wasn't a strike, the truth, I was teaching them how to adjust. Not to just pitches, but to who was in control of balls and strikes. The umpire. The message was immediate and clear: We don't practice in ideal conditions only. We practice for the worst-case scenarios, too.

Three Rounds, Infinite Learning

We had just added critical variability to our practice. From that day forward, anytime a player entered my cage, one of three rounds was applied:

ROUND #1: Damage Zone Round (Less Than Two Strikes) - Hunt your pitch only; Anything outside your damage zone = take it; Weak contact = you're out of the cage; Purpose: Develop discipline, pitch selection and intent.

ROUND #2: Bad Umpire Round (Expanded Zone) - Chalk line extends the plate; Swing at anything between chalk and plate; Takes in the expanded zone = you're out; Purpose: Develop adaptability to game conditions.

ROUND #3: Hit-and-Run Round (Contact Required) - Must put the ball in play regardless of location; Swing at anything close; Miss or weak pop-up = you're out; Purpose: Develop bat-to-ball skills and situational hitting.

Each player didn't know which round they were getting until they stepped in the box. Sometimes I'd announce it. Sometimes I wouldn't. They were there to learn how to hit, in all conditions, against all challenges.

The Logic Nobody Talks About

Here's what I finally came to understand: If the average number of pitches during an at-bat is five, what's the average number of pitches we give players in the cage? Twenty? Thirty? Fifty? If I want players to become disciplined, am I developing discipline in the cage?

For years, the answer was no. I was giving them volume. I was giving them comfort. I was giving them confidence built on a foundation of grooved pitches that would never exist in competition from the better pitch callers and pitchers. This is what I finally understood: I was the problem. We were not developing in the cage what I wanted demonstrated in competition.

HONESTY MOMENT

Count the last 10 cage sessions you ran (or participated in): How many pitches per round? How many different locations? How many consequences for poor decisions? What were you actually teaching: swinging or hitting? Your answers reveal whether you're training zoo tigers or jungle hunters.

That's when the metaphor hit me like one of those grooved pitches I'd been throwing...

The Zoo Tiger Problem

It was like training tigers in the zoo for survival in the jungle. Sure, the tiger looks impressive in the controlled environment. It can perform tricks. It responds to cues. The zookeepers feel great about the tiger's progress. But put that tiger in the jungle, where conditions change, where threats come from unexpected angles, where there are no grooved meals, and suddenly, all that cage training means nothing.

> My players were zoo tigers. They
> looked great in practice where I
> threw them pitches they could crush
> but in games with bad umpires, with
> pitchers who lived off the plate, with
> speeds they hadn't seen, with
> pressure they hadn't felt, they were
> unprepared.

The ten-year-old pitcher who lived down and away? He exposed me, not my players. He revealed that my training was incomplete. I had taught them to hit in ideal conditions while ignoring the reality that competition is never ideal.

WHEN THE MAGIC HAPPENED

The Player Who Walked Out

About two weeks into the new system, during a Damage Zone round with less than two strikes, a young man with a low damage zone received a high pitch. He crushed it. Absolutely demolished it, the hardest ball hit in practice that day. Right after contact, with three pitches remaining in his round, he turned around and walked out of the cage. That was his first pitch.

I stood there, watching him walk to the back of the line. My first instinct was to call him back: "Hey, you've got three more swings!" I didn't say anything. I realized what had just happened: The discipline and accountability were no longer being imposed by me. The players had internalized it.

He had just chosen his identity over reps. He'd recognized a pitch outside his damage zone, crushed it for power since his body started reacting, though then immediately walked away rather than waste time chasing pitches that weren't his. The other players in line watched him. Nobody laughed. Nobody said, "What are you doing?" They understood. That's when I knew something special was happening. I knew these players were about to make some pitchers very uncomfortable. I also knew these were going to be future high school stars in the state of Mississippi.

The Starkville Tournament

Our next tournament was in Starkville, Mississippi. We were matched up against a good-looking pitcher who, during warmups, located well down and away consistently. After he faced the first right-handed hitter in our lineup, his in-game location was down and away, just like warmups. I walked over to the dugout and told the entire team: "Bad umpire round, guys."

That was our code. It meant: "This umpire is calling low-and-away strikes, or the pitcher is located there, so expand your zone appropriately. Still hunt your damage zones first, just know the zone is bigger today." This ten-year-old group applied game planning, discipline, and adaptability. At the end of the game, we had nine hard-hit balls to the right field grass, all of them because we practiced expanding our zone with the chalk line. To this day, it is one of the most magnificent coaching experiences I have encountered.

MLB VALIDATION AND PARENT BACKLASH

The Conversation With Corey Dickerson

A couple years later, I shared this 10u hitting approach with Corey Dickerson, at the time a six-year MLB veteran and All-Star. Corey's response stopped me cold. "I didn't understand that concept of hitting until I was a professional." This was shocking to hear. Then again, we're talking about MLB, it takes enormous talent to make it that far. However, MLB players understand something most youth coaches don't: The better the pitching, the better your approach needs to be. And the foundation of a great approach starts with discipline.

This was the greatest motivation I could have ever received moving forward. Unlike what you see on the internet or social media, swing clips and launch angle debates, the majority of my conversations with Corey have been about approaching pitchers, pillar number 1. Not mechanics. Approach. With the validation of an MLB All-Star, I knew I was onto something.

Here's what struck me most: Corey Dickerson is describing the exact same principle I was teaching 10-year-olds, know your damage zone and hunt it relentlessly. That conversation confirmed everything. If MLB players need approach and discipline to survive against the best pitching in the world, why do we teach 10-year-olds that volume and reps are enough?

The Parent Backlash

Unfortunately, my dreams of developing the best high school hitters in Mississippi came to an abrupt end. My buddy, the head coach, called me to share. "I've got a problem," he said. "A few parents are threatening to leave if you come back next season." "Why?" I asked, though I already knew. "They say we're not winning enough. They want more cage time. They want their kids to get more swings." There it was.

I was getting fired from a 10u baseball team, not because the kids weren't improving, but because I refused to run a cage bomb factory. The parents wanted their sons to feel good. I wanted their sons to get well. We wanted different things.

Another ego crush. Now, here's what I've learned: God closes some doors to keep you from going into rooms He wants you out of. And did He ever close this one with purpose? A few weeks later, a softball coach called. That call led me to LP, to Lana, to understanding that the lessons those 10-year-olds taught me would apply to even Power 5 athletes.

The parents wanted cage bombs. God wanted me in a different environment. I'm grateful He closed that door.

The Softball Revelation

I knew going into this position as the hitting coordinator, to lean on my instructor skills. Just like all strikes are not made equal, neither are all players.

I entered the role of this position with more game sense and cage sense.

Applying The System To Softball

Everything works the same. Here's what changes: In softball, the "up" zone is the rise ball zone. The "down" zone is the drop/change zone. In addition, I understood my job wasn't to fix their weakness yet. It's to identify their strength and let them dominate it. After all, practice times with travel ball teams have very little to no practice time. Therefore, I had to coach more hitting than the swing.

Why This Matters More For Softball

THE PROBLEM: Your player with the .450 average? She's about to face a college pitcher who throws: Up to 68 mph rise that moves 8 inches, 59 mph curve with late break, 52 mph change with 10 inches of drop, and up to 65 mph screw that runs inside.

If she's never practiced damage zones and speed differentials, she's hitting .200 or less her freshman year. If there are at-bat opportunities her freshman year. With three years remaining to do what she loves. Then it is all over.

THE TRUTH: Nothing happened to her swing. Her swing was always fine. She just never learned to hit. Softball demands even more discipline than baseball. Same principles. Higher demand. They don't move on to the minor or major leagues for additional development. This is it! Softball players require more of the truth.

STOP THE CAGE BOMBS. START THE HARD TRUTHS. Your players' college careers depend on it.

The hardest truth of all: Teaching approach and swing is the easy part. What comes next is harder. Because now you have to answer the question every parent, player, and coach will ask: "What makes a hitter actually discipline themselves to hunt their pitch when everyone else is swinging at everything?"

That answer, the first two pillars of hitting, changes everything. It's the reason two players with identical swings produce completely different results. It's the reason your best practice hitter becomes your worst game hitter. You can't see it on video. You can't measure it with technology. You can't fix it with more reps. But without it, everything else you've taught them is worthless.

The Bridge To Chapter 3

You've just discovered the difference between batting practice and hitting development in a team environment. You've learned that five pitches with consequences beat fifty-five pitches with none. You understand that cage bombs feel good but fix nothing.

Here's the problem: You can implement every method in this chapter. You can stop the cage bombs. You can introduce consequences. You can create game-like environments. You can teach your players to hunt their damage zones and take disciplined swings. But some will still fail.

Not because their swing broke. Not because they didn't understand the approach. Not because they weren't disciplined. They just didn't believe. The belief of facing pitchers starts with three pillars.

Two have already been referenced:

PILLAR 1: DECISION - Knowing what pitch to hunt before it's thrown.

PILLAR 2: DISCIPLINE - Having the courage to take a strike in your weak zone to get a pitch in your strong zone. Or TAKE a fast ball right down the middle when you were sitting on a slow change.

The third pillar? It's the one everyone teaches. The one you see on video. The one that distracts us from the first two. But it's the reason a player with a perfect swing and no approach still goes 0-for-4. It's the reason two players with identical mechanics produce completely different results. It's the reason your best practice hitter becomes your worst game hitter. It's the reason a college scout will watch a player crush it in the cage and still say, "She won't make it at our level."

The Invisible Game

You can't measure it with technology. You can't fix it with more mechanical focused reps. You can't teach it with drills. But without it, everything you just learned in this chapter is worthless.

What good is knowing your damage zone if you don't make the right decision for what is expected? What good is having discipline if you don't believe your approach will work when you're 0-for-2 in the championship game? What good is taking fifty-five high-quality swings in the cage, if your lack of decision and discipline doesn't create that damage swing?

The Belief System

In Chapter 1, you learned the difference between swing and hitting. In Chapter 2, you learned the difference between cage bombs and real development. In Chapter 3, you're about to learn the difference between players who have the tools and players who have the belief to use them under pressure. But if you think belief is just "positive thinking" or "confidence" or "mental toughness," you're wrong. It's deeper. It's more complex. It's more powerful. It's the reason most talented players never reach their potential.

The Story You Need To Hear

Two players, same age, same level of talent, and nearly identical swings.

Player A: Crushed in every cage session. Heard the term approach. Had no discipline. Didn't understand her damage zones.

Player B: Every pitch had an approach. Had discipline. Knew her damage zones.

Player A went on to hit .180. Player B goes off in and out of the conference. What was the difference? Not the swing. Not the approach. Not the discipline. The difference was the intentional preparation.

In Chapter 3, I'm going to show you exactly what that means, and how to build it in yourself or your players before it's too late.

The Hardest Truth Of All

You can fix a swing in... months. You can teach an approach in... weeks. You can develop discipline in... days.

You've just discovered that cage bombs are lying to you. Five pitches with consequences beat fifty-five pitches with none. Comfort is the enemy of competition, but even if you eliminate cage bombs and create consequences in practice, there's still something missing.

Here's what nobody tells you: you can have perfect practice methods and still fail in games. You can stop the cage bombs, create discipline, and simulate pressure... and still go 0-for-4. Why? Because practice methods are only half the equation. They teach you HOW to train, but they don't teach you WHAT to develop.

You've been training without a target. You've been working hard without knowing what "good" actually looks like. Putting in the hours without understanding what separates college stars from college bench players.

In the next chapter, you're going to discover the three pillars that determine whether you thrive or survive at the next level. These aren't all mechanical pillars. They're not physical pillars. They're the three elements that every elite hitter possesses, and most good hitters are missing.

Alana Johnson understood these pillars before her first college at-bat. Most players don't discover them until their junior year, if they discover them at all. The three pillars changed Alana's trajectory from recruited player to Women's College World Series starter. Will you wait until it's too late to learn them?

CHAPTER 3

THE THREE PILLARS OF A HITTER

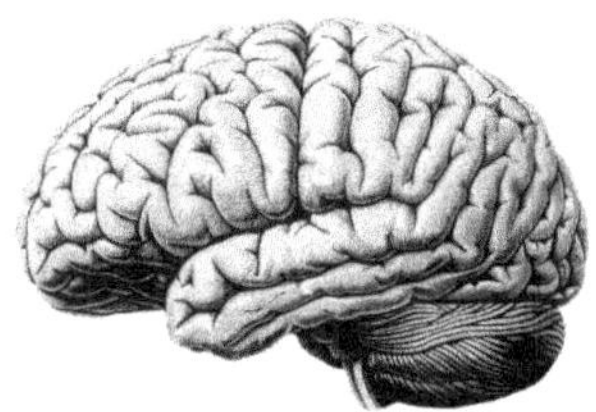

Decision, Discipline, and Damage

"You will play at the next level. If you want to be GREAT at the next level, you must understand that all strikes are not made equal." - January 8, 2019, the cage session that changed everything

THE RUDE AWAKENING

You've been crushing it for years. High school star. Travel ball legend. Middle of the order. Stats that made coaches' jaws drop. You carried the label everywhere you went: "One of the best." Then you step on a college campus and everything you thought you knew gets stripped away in about two weeks.

The Problem

You're convinced your swing is the answer. After all, it's worked for years, hasn't it? You've spent countless hours in the cage perfecting your positions, drilling mechanics, obsessing over every millimeter of your bat path. You arrive at college thinking, "I've got this."

Here's what you don't realize: the gap has closed. You're not special anymore. Everyone around you was a star. Everyone has decorated walls and filled stat sheets. Everyone is just as hungry as you. Your talent, by itself, isn't the separator anymore. Many will not be told this truth.

The Truth

The biggest shift isn't talent, it's exposure. Exposing you to what you don't do well. Your new coach already knows your weaknesses. They weren't discovered this week. Not even at your first practice. They were logged months, maybe years earlier during your recruitment.

That rise ball you chase out of the zone? Noted. That curveball that makes you roll over? Remembered. That screwball with velocity that you hit off the handle? Already in the scouting report. Not to mention, the defenses are also much better. Players are bigger, faster and stronger! If somehow your holes weren't discovered before you arrived, they will be. The pitchers you now face aren't throwing to help you "look good" like you do in the cage. Even your college teammates are trained to exploit you if the pitching coach has identified that swing vulnerability.

Think about that. Your own teammates know how to beat you. The pitching machine is not set up right down the middle either. If you believe your swing alone will carry you through, you're about to face a brutal reality check. This is where understanding Decision, Discipline, and Damage, together, can transform you from surviving to thriving.

THE THREE PILLARS OF HITTING

PILLAR ONE: DECISION-MAKING

THE Napkin That Changed My Coaching Forever

Let me take you to Nashville. 2017. Pitch-A-Palooza. Front row. A gentleman leaned over and asked me a question that would reshape everything I thought I knew about hitting: "Are you familiar with a term called effective velocity?" "No sir," I responded. He grabbed a napkin and drew a strike zone. Then added a diagonal line from the northwest corner to the southeast corner.

"The up-and-in corner," he explained, "represents the fastest area. Add about four miles per hour to the effective velocity." I stared at that napkin. "So, a 60-mph fastball up and in..." "Feels like 64 mph," he finished. "And down-and-away? That same 60 mph pitch feels like 56." YOU HAVE TO BE KIDDING ME. ALL STRIKES ARE NOT MADE EQUAL NOW HAS A DEEPER MEANING.

Hitters really have to be strategic, I thought! Before I could even leave Nashville, I was on the phone with Perry Husband, the discoverer of effective velocity. "Tell me more!" Suddenly, I had a completely different understanding of how pitchers disrupt timing. I can now help hitters make much better decisions.

The Problem with Decision Making Strategies

How do you make decisions at the plate? Most players I ask don't have a clear answer. Here are the responses I hear most often: "Swing at strikes," "Look for my pitch," "Assess how the pitcher is attacking hitters like me," "Whatever plan the coach gives me," "Hit behind the runner."

Let me break down why each of these approaches is incomplete, or flat-out wrong.

The "Swing at Strikes" Illusion

If six fastballs only at 60 mph can fit in each of the nine zones of the strike zone, that means 54 balls can fit inside the strike zone. I'm not even counting the edges or contact points out front or deep in the zone. That's at least 54 different contact points related to early or late timing, and up or down barrel position. Only one pitch. Now throw in the fact that you'll be early and late on pitches, congratulations, you just changed the speeds yourself! Thanks, says the pitcher.

Now consider this: the same fastball on the outer edge is slower than the pitch on the inner edge. Couple that with up-and-in versus down-and-away, and suddenly you're not dealing with one speed, you're dealing with a spectrum. Now, let me paint you the full picture of what you're actually facing from an effective velocity perspective:

Table 3.0 - Pitch location and speed feel

Pitch	Location	Radar Speed	Feels Like (EV)
Drop	Down & In	60 mph	60 mph
Drop	Down & Away	60 mph	56 mph
Rise	Up & In	60 mph	64 mph
Rise	Up & Away	60 mph	60 mph
Curve	Middle-Away	60 mph	57 mph
Screw	Middle-In	60 mph	62 mph

Look at that carefully. The same 60 mph drop ball can feel faster or slower depending on location. The same 60 mph rise ball ranges from 60-64 mph in effective velocity. Now think about your current approach. If you're "looking for the drop," which drop are you looking for? The 56-mph version or the 61-mph version? Because your timing must be completely different.

Let's Stop And Think

This is not rocket science. Ask any of your players these four questions: A 60-mph pitch inside, what is your timing? A 60-mph pitch away, what is your timing? Are all strikes made equal? Can you have the same timing for both locations and produce the same power?

The Barrel Position Factor

Here's another layer you probably haven't considered: the position of your barrel at contact. For pitches at the top of the zone, your barrel should be closer to a flat position. Pitches down in the zone require a more angled or steeper barrel position. It's perfectly okay to swing at strikes. If you have a timing hole or a path hole in your swing, your hard contact opportunities get reduced in the areas you don't hit well.

This is especially critical if you're not the most talented player on the field. You may have to use a lot more of your 90% (mind) and less of your 10% (body).

The "Look For My Pitch" Confusion

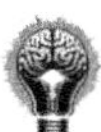

How often have you heard a coach say, "Swing at your pitch"? Now let me ask you: What is your pitch? Is a curve at 64 mph and a curve at 55 mph both your pitch? Or is a curve at 60 mph and a fastball outside at 60 mph in the same location your pitch? What about the same pitch type at three different speeds, 55 mph, 60 mph, 65 mph? Are they all your pitch?

Here's what I've found: even at the college level, most players don't have clarity about what they do well. They have a much better understanding of what they don't do well. The challenge is this: your pitch isn't just a type. It's a specific speed AND location combination, because you need to understand how to manipulate your timing. Players get confused when the speed gets faster or slower, even if it's the same pitch they "handle well."

The "Watch How Others Get Pitched" Mistake

This is one of my favorite flawed approaches: basing your decision on how pitchers attacked other hitters on the same side of the plate. You've probably done this for years. I'm still trying to figure out how it works.

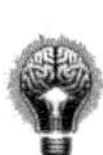

Think about it: the average player takes swings off a tee, and hits flips down the middle to prepare for a game. Then they get to the game and ask their teammate, "What is she throwing?" or "What is her pitch doing?" Really? Wouldn't it make more sense to work on those answers, via scouting report, BEFORE you face the pitcher? Like a few days before?

What do you think about these pre-game questions: What will she throw? How fast will she throw? Where does she locate? How much does it move?

Consider this. All programs don't have access to the same scouting tools. This limited or no access does not prevent you from game planning ahead of time.

Here's the bigger issue: you may have a different load, rhythm, and stride than your teammate. So how can you make a decision based on someone who moves and times pitches completely differently than you do? You're trying to navigate with someone else's map.

The "Hit Behind The Runner" Fantasy

This isn't golf. The ball isn't sitting on a stationary tee. When hitting off a golf tee or batting tee, you don't have to deal with: Vertical-horizontal breaks, Fast-slow speeds, Up-and-in, up-and-away, Down-and-in, down-and-away variabilities.

Yes, talented players can manipulate the direction of batted balls. It often comes with a sacrifice of exit velocity. Those who can do it the best are the most talented. If that's going to be the trade-off, maybe there should be more attention given to bunting.

Players have a hard enough time squaring up what they know is coming. Now you want the average player to manipulate location while facing the best pitcher in the district that is throwing vertical or horizontal break, and change of speed? What are your real chances with a pitch inside and trying to hit it the other way?

The Truth

Let me show you something that will make this crystal clear.

CHALLENGE #1: THE HEAT MAP REVELATION - Go to BaseballSavant.com right now. Pick any MLB player. Look up their batting average against fastballs greater than 97 mph versus less than 95 mph. Then pull up their zone profile.

Before reading further, do this:

Go to BaseballSavant.com

Click Search > Major League Search

Select Player Type: Batter

Choose a metric range: greater than 97 mph

Enter a player's name

Click Search > Graph > Zone Profile > BA.

An example are the 2025 season batting averages for Matt Olson in three categories: all pitches, all fastballs, and fastballs greater than 90 mph.

Table 3.1 - Zone, pitch type and speed comparisons (source www.baseballsavant.mlb.com)

Zone	Location	All Pitches	Fastballs	Fastballs > 95 mph
1	Up-Away	.091	.087	.000
2	Up-Middle	.279	.265	.182
3	Up-In	.231	.250	.333
4	Mid-Away	.261	.176	.250
5	Mid-Mid	.443	.545	.444
6	Mid-In	.404	.412	.474
7	Down-Away	.228	.250	.200
8	Down-Middle	.303	.308	.231
9	Down-In	.410	.529	.500
11	NS-Up/Out	.154	.083	.125
12	NS-Up/In	.176	.200	.300
13	NS-Down/Out	.148	.429	.500
14	NS-Down/In	.208	.216	.077

NS-Not a strike. Do MLB players, the best in the world, have the same batting average in all nine zones? Of course not. So, before you continue, answer this question. Are all fastballs strikes made the same?

If the best players in the world have different success rates in different zones and with different speeds, what makes you think you're any different? What advantage does a player who hits low strikes well have if they're looking for elevated strikes? You'd be setting yourself up for failure even if you know what's coming, if your body can't position the barrel in that part of the zone without cheating. There's a great chance you don't even know how to cheat to spots in order to give your barrel a chance. What if each player in the line up has a natural barrel approach, or cheat to the spot approach?

The Value Of Customized Approaches

Here's what I will argue: there is tremendous value in a coach understanding the strengths of each hitter in advance. When a pitcher moves the ball around the strike zone, imagine if each hitter's plan was assigned based on where their barrel path naturally comes through the zone. How much more difficult would that be for pitching coaches to game plan against?

"If coaches give you what pitchers do, you have a better chance doing what you do." Does this work in real competition?

The Decision In Action

Once you understand effective velocity, barrel positioning, and your own strengths, you can make informed decisions BEFORE the pitch is thrown. You're not reacting to what you see. You're acting on what you've prepared for. This is the first pillar: Decision-Making. You decide what speed and location you're hunting. You decide what your body and barrel need to do to attack that pitch. You decide your plan before you ever step in the box.

But making the right decision is only the beginning...

PILLAR TWO: DISCIPLINE

THE TALENT TRAP

The Player You Know

You know these players. You've watched them since they were six years old. Always the best. Always ahead of everyone else. Always getting away with everything.

That kid who makes the play but not the right way and still gets praised. That player who can swing at anything and somehow make it work. That athlete who doesn't have to adjust until the playoffs or faces their equal talent on the mound or circle. At the time, nobody can challenge them. You know exactly who I'm talking about. That was Bryce.

The Problem

I'd been working with Bryce since he was ten. Tremendous talent. Natural ability that most players would kill for. But talent creates its own prison. When you've dominated your entire life, discipline becomes your greatest weakness. Why take pitches when you can hit everything? Why have an approach when "see ball, hit ball" has always worked? Success becomes the enemy of development.

The Cage Session

On this particular day, we were running the Damage Zone round. The rules were clear: Hunt your damage zone only. Take anything outside it with less than two strikes. Weak contact = you're out. Bryce wouldn't do it. Strike after strike came outside his damage zone. Strike after strike, he swung. This wasn't random. He'd just finished a tournament where he struggled. His confidence was shaken. So his instinct was to swing at everything, to prove he could still hit. That's exactly when discipline matters most.

The Truth

I stopped the round. "Bryce, I know what your problem is." He looked at me. "What's that?" "Your problem is you're too good." Silence. "Right now, you're too talented for your competition. You can get away with swinging at anything because the pitching isn't good enough to make you pay for bad decisions."

I let that sink in. "Now here's what's coming: In a few years, you'll face a pitcher committed to a Power 5 program. He's throwing 93 mph up-and-in with an 86 mph slider. If you swing at everything like you're doing right now, he's going to embarrass you." Bryce didn't like hearing it. Nobody does.

"So you have a choice," I continued. "Learn discipline now, in this cage, where the consequences are low, or let that Power 5 pitcher teach you the lesson later, when a college coach is watching and your scholarship might depend on it."

The Uncomfortable Reality

Talented players like Bryce have the hardest time watching strikes go by. Why? Because swinging has always worked. Because their hand-eye coordination has always bailed them out. Because nobody's ever made them pay for being undisciplined. Until someone does. By then, it's too late.

The Lesson For Instructors

If you're working with talented players, you have to tell them the truth they don't want to hear. The day you meet someone equally talented in the circle or on the mound, your talent won't be enough. That day is coming. The only question is whether they'll be ready for it. Discipline isn't about being patient. It's about being smart enough to know that the rules change when the competition gets better. Bryce learned that lesson in the cage. Most players learn it on the bench. When we refuse to tell the truth, you are lying to them.

HONESTY MOMENT

If you're a talented player reading this, ask yourself: Do I swing at pitches outside my damage zone because I can, or because I should? Am I developing discipline now, or hoping my talent will always be enough? What happens when I face a pitcher just as talented?

Your answers determine whether you dominate at the next level or sit on the bench wondering what happened. Talent gets you noticed. Discipline gets you playing time. Which one are you working on?

THE CAGE SESSION THAT CHANGED EVERYTHING

January 8, 2019. Tuesday night. That's when Lana Johnson walked into the cage. I'd already watched her play. I'd competed against her as a pitch caller. I knew immediately: this was special talent. However, talent alone wouldn't be enough for where she was headed. Before she swung at one pitch in the cage, I spoke these words to her: "You will play at the next level," I told her. "If you want to be great at the next level, you must understand that all strikes are not made equal."

The Problem

When you hear the word "discipline," you're probably thinking about strike zone discipline. Swinging at strikes. Laying off balls. That's what everyone thinks, but you're missing something critical. God had blessed Lana with extraordinary hand-eye coordination. Her swing didn't need major changes. Just tweaks here and there. However, without understanding the inequality of the strike zone, even her talent would hit a ceiling.

Most cage sessions sound exactly the same. You hear cues about the swing: "Keep your hands inside." "Stay through the middle." "Get your hips through." How often do you hear about hunting speed? About stalking location? About the deliberate practice of timing pitches on the edges?

The Truth

The real discipline isn't just about swinging at strikes. It's about knowing which strikes give you the best chance to do damage. Think of the strike zone like a buffet. Sure, all the food is technically edible. Are you going to load your plate with everything? Some dishes will fuel your performance, and while others will weigh you down.

For Lana, every cage session became intentional. Every pitch had a purpose. We worked all corners, all changes of speed. Sometimes we'd adjust a position or a move. Most of the emphasis was placed on position and timing based on pitch location. When she wasn't disciplined, we let her know it. "Sounds like 90% and 10% again." So, here's what really separated Lana from everyone else...

The Real Separator

It wasn't the discovery of her specific needs. It was the intentional reps in the cage back home with Chad, her father. When entering the cage with a purpose, Lana was held accountable to the specific zone they were working that day. When there was a swing outside the area she was hunting, Chad would ask one of two questions: "What are we working on?" Or: "Were you looking for that?"

Two simple questions. They forced clarity. They demanded intention. They built a disciplined mindset. Think about your own cage sessions. How many swings do you take without a specific purpose? How many times do you swing at something you weren't hunting just because it was close?

The goal was to assist her in being good at the next level. Not feeling good at the current time.

Lana's Freshman Transformation

Lana entered her freshman year at the University of Washington. Like most freshmen, there was a challenging transition. Everyone is good or better. You're facing better coaches and better pitchers. The season started, and like most freshmen, she had her challenges. In college, you don't get as many at-bats to work through struggles.

Just before conference season started, she had a conversation with the staff about her comfort level with approach and scouting information. Lana went from fishing for pitches to hunting them. That "90%:10%" again. She made DECISIONS about what pitches to hunt. She had the DISCIPLINE to stick to those decisions, even when other strikes were available.

This is where the first two pillars come together:

> Decision without Discipline = You know what you should hunt, nevertheless you chase everything anyway. Discipline without Decision = You lay off pitches outside the strike but still you have no plan inside the zone.

Even the best plan falls apart without the third pillar...

CHALLENGE #2: THE ACCOUNTABILITY AUDIT

For your next three cage sessions, bring someone with you who will hold you accountable: What speed you're hunting, What location you're working, What you'll do if you swing outside that zone. Have them ask you those questions every time you chase. Write down your answers. See how quickly your discipline improves when someone's watching.

PILLAR THREE: DAMAGE

THE POWER PARADOX

Everyone loves the long ball, right?

The Problem

Everyone wants to hit the long ball. Very few put in the time with a strength and conditioning coach who understands overhand rotational athletes. The best strength and conditioning coaches (not certified trainers) know: What muscles to target, When to target them, The proper dosage. Doing damage requires explosive movement of the body, which includes a combination of speed and strength.

I find it interesting that the new bat gets all the attention for power, while the body is ignored. The body gets the attention for hitting mechanics, while the mind is ignored.

The Truth

Think of your body like a car engine. You can have the best driver in the world (your decision-making), the best steering and handling (your discipline), though if the engine doesn't have the horsepower, you're not winning many races. Power isn't just about swinging hard. It's about: POSITION (Where your body is set up to deliver force), TIMING (When you unleash that force in relation to pitch location), and ROTATION (Your body's ability to generate and transfer explosive energy).

The Barrel Position Reality

Let's connect this back to decision-making. Remember how we talked about the barrel needing different positions for different parts of the zone? For pitches at the top of the zone, your barrel should be closer to flat. For pitches down in the zone, you need a more angled or steeper barrel.

The catch: your body must rotate and coordinate enough to get into those positions without sacrificing bat speed to do damage up or down. If you can't generate enough force from a steeper position, guess what happens when you're forced to hit low pitches? You either: Try to manipulate your path and lose power, keep your natural path and make weak contact, or miss the pitch entirely.

This level of manipulation only adds to the complexity of hitting the round ball that may have vertical or horizontal breaks and fast or slow speeds. This is why "hit behind the runner" drives me crazy.

CHALLENGE #3: THE POWER AUDIT

For the next two weeks, honestly assess: How many days do you spend in the weight room versus the cage? Does your strength coach understand rotational athletes? Can you generate the same bat speed from a steep barrel position as you can from a flat one? Do you know your exit velocity in different parts of the zone?

Write down your answers. Then ask yourself: Am I really preparing to do damage, or am I just hoping my swing shows up?

The Synergy Of The Three Pillars

These three pillars don't work independently. You can have incredible discipline, conversely without proper decision-making, you're hunting the wrong pitches in the wrong zones. You can make great decisions about which pitches to attack, in contrast without the damage component, the strength, athleticism, and explosive power, you're hitting weak ground balls on your "pitch." You can have all the physical power in the world (damage), on the other hand, without discipline and decision-making, you're swinging at pitches you have no chance of hitting the ball hard.

It's like a three-legged stool. Remove one leg and everything collapses.

The 90%:10% Principle Revealed

You've seen this phrase throughout the chapter. Let me make it clear:

> 90% = Your Mind (Decision + Discipline), 10% = Your Body (Damage). Most players spend 90% of their time working on the 10%.

They obsess over their swing mechanics. They take endless reps in the cage with no purpose. They chase the newest bat or the latest hitting gadget.

The elite players? They flip the script. They spend most of their preparation working on their 90%: Understanding their strengths and weaknesses, studying pitcher tendencies, practicing deliberate, intentional reps with specific purposes, and training their minds to make better decisions faster. Then they supplement with the 10%: building the strength and athleticism to deliver damage, and fine-tuning mechanics to maximize their natural abilities.

Your Turn

You're standing at a crossroads right now. You can keep doing what you've always done, taking mindless reps, hoping your talent shows up, and reacting to whatever the pitcher gives you, or you can embrace these three pillars and transform yourself into a complete hitter.

FINAL CHALLENGE: THE 7-DAY COMMITMENT

For the next seven days:

DECISION: Before every cage session or game, identify: Your best zone (speed + location), Your plan if the pitcher stays away from that zone, How you'll recognize your pitch.

DISCIPLINE: Hold yourself accountable: Name what you're hunting before every pitch, if you swing outside your zone, acknowledge it out loud, Track how many "disciplined" swings you take versus total swings.

DAMAGE: Invest in your power: Spend at least 3 days in the weight room with a proven strength and conditioning coach. test your exit velocity in different zones, Work on generating bat speed from uncomfortable barrel positions.

At the end of seven days, answer this question: Are you a swinger who reacts to the game, or a hitter who dictates it? The choice has always been yours.

Now you understand what elite hitters have always known: the three pillars aren't optional, they're essential. In the next chapter, we'll dive deep into how to actually train these pillars through specific drills and mental exercises. You'll discover the exact cage routines that transformed Lana and dozens of other players from overlooked freshmen into impact performers. First, you need to understand one more critical concept that ties everything together…

You now understand the three pillars: Decision, Discipline, and Damage. You know that hitting is 90% from the neck up and 10% from the neck down. So here's the question that should be haunting you right now: If hitting is 90% mental, why do you spend 90% of your training obsessing over measurements that only capture the 10%?

Walk into any cage in America right now. What do you see? Kinematic sequence reports. Ball exit speed readouts. Launch angle graphs. Angular velocity measurements. Ground force data. Players drowning in numbers, convinced that if they just measure enough things, they'll unlock the secret to hitting.

The uncomfortable truth that's about to explode everything you think you know about data: The players with the best numbers in the cage often have the worst results in games. The hitters with "perfect" kinematic sequences struggle against quality pitching. The athletes with the highest exit velocities sit on the bench while "uglier" swingers drive in runs.

Why? Because you're measuring the wrong things. You're collecting fancy data that impresses nobody and ignoring functional data that wins games. In the next chapter, you're going to discover why your $10,000 technology might not be what you need. Why the data that matters most can be captured on your phone. Why the drive home from a random practice session revealed more truth than a thousand sensor readings.

This chapter will challenge every assumption you have about measurement, progress, and what actually makes hitters better. It might just save you thousands of dollars and hundreds of wasted hours.

CHAPTER 4

BEYOND BALL EXIT SPEED

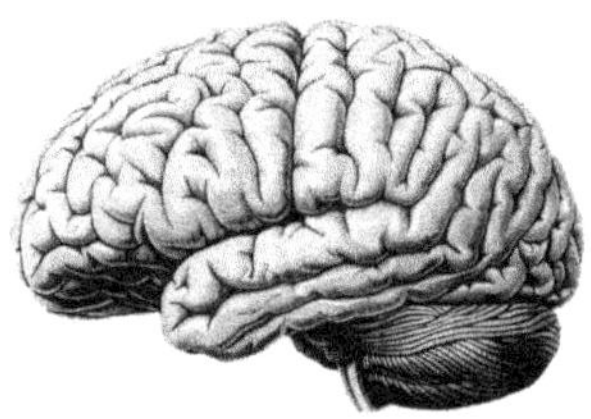

Functional Data vs. Fancy Data

"Fancy data impresses. Functional data improves. Most coaches choose the wrong one." - Coaching Wisdom

THE RABBIT HOLE

"We measure the body, bat, and ball." Jeff Hargar told me in 2019. At the time, he was Arizona State's Hitting Coach. Those seven words sent me down a rabbit hole so deep, I wasn't sure when, or if I'd return to the surface. This is where I discovered the kinematic sequence: the measurement of pelvis, thoracic, arm, and bat angular velocity. I dove into technology that could monitor how well-hit balls were compared to how the body moved. My ability to measure and understand measuring the body, bat and ball has been essential to simplifying *individual* player development.

Very important to address Pillar #3: Damage. I paid close attention to specific metrics: The sequencing of each segment (pelvis, torso, arm, hand), Angular velocity (because I'd always been "told" it's about body speed and bat speed), Ball exit speed (how can you assess a player without this, right?), and Launch angle (you can't be a hitting coach without checking this, right?).

I prioritized what the industry put in front of us all. That's what we do in softball and baseball. We listen to what the experts say, and we do exactly what they say. We don't question it. Then a thought occurred on a drive home I never heard anyone discuss...

THE AWAKENING

THE DRIVE HOME THAT CHANGED MY COACHING

You know those moments when random thoughts collide and suddenly everything becomes clear? That's what happened to me on a random drive home. The thoughts came rapid-fire: The kinematic sequence measures players who aren't committed to a workout regime. I'm only looking at baseline data. These metrics will all change as they get older and more committed to improving strength and becoming more explosive.

Wait... maybe the data can be used to expedite buy-in once numbers improve following a drill. That could work. Hold on, when movers are categorized as "loose" or "tight," shouldn't the increase in angular velocity from pelvis to thoracic differ between them? What about degrees of hip and shoulder separation? Yes, separation occurs in all hitters, though not at the same differential.

A critical question hit me: If I'm forcing this separation on players who move more like two hinges on a door, could I be doing more damage than good? Another thought crashed in: How efficient is my time improving these measurements when, at the level of players I work with, most of what I need to see can be evaluated directly from my phone?

If I understand my cage dimensions, I can determine if the ball was hit in the air too much. Even if I can't, we can review the video from the phone. The player and I can come to the same conclusion. There's no debate about a ground ball.

The Problem

You've fallen into the same trap I did. You're chasing numbers. Metrics. Data points. You've got: Kinematic sequence reports,

Angular velocity charts, Ball exit speed readouts, Launch angle graphs, and attack angle measurements and yet you're drowning in information and yet you are starving for clarity.

You've invested thousands in technology. You spend half your cage time setting up equipment, calibrating sensors, downloading apps. Players stand around waiting while you troubleshoot Bluetooth connections. Meanwhile, the obvious problems are staring you right in the face:

- Torso too far back → impacting bat path and quality of contact
- Torso too far forward → impacting bat path and quality of contact
- Late timing → impacting quality of contact and path
- Early timing → impacting quality of contact and path
- Inconsistent tempo → impacting timing, quality of contact, and path.

You don't need a $10,000 device to see these. You need your eyes first.

The Truth

After collecting these thoughts on that drive home, I realized something profound: These devices were starting to interfere with the main thing: addressing the obvious. Think about it like this: imagine you're trying to help someone improve their golf game. You could use: Launch monitors, Swing speed radars, Club path sensors, Ball spin analyzers. Or... you could watch them swing and notice they're falling backward on every drive. Do you need these tools for the obvious?

The simplicity revelation hit me hard: most improvement could be viewed right on my phone. If the player wasn't in their balanced position, I could see it. An imbalance results in a distortion in the kinematic sequence. I could tell if the player was early or late. When your timing is off, you won't be in a balanced position, which reduces power and adversely impacts the kinematic sequence. When the bat isn't squaring the ball up, there's a reduction in ball exit speed. Rhythm and tempo, when disrupted, impact everything: timing, sequencing, ground force, path, and adjustability.

Don't *misunderstand* me, measurement tools have their place. They were just not essential to my players and the areas of improvement they needed. These tools were becoming a distraction to me and, at times, to the players.

The Simplicity Principle

All I needed was to: watch the body prior to rotation, monitor bat path coming through the zone, and watch ball flight after contact. If the swing got faster and more efficient, I'd just go to the video. Slow motion shows you most of what you need.

What I look for: Lead shoulder up prior to the front foot landing, torso leaning forward or back prior to rotation, Barrel casting prior to rotation, Torso leaning over the plate prior to rotation, Jerky rhythm, Bat path crossing the ball path line, up or down, Ball flight after contact (square or cut), Intentional extension of the stride leg, Rotation prior to stabilization of the lead leg, Pushing of the hands versus releasing the barrel, Shrugging of the shoulder. Just to name a few.

The key is possessing the skill to identify the root cause of what's impacting the desired outcome: squaring the round ball up with the round bat and hitting it hard. When these two things happen, we make it tough on the defense. In addition, the data will improve. Here's where some instructors, and maybe you, get this completely wrong...

THE CAGE STAR PROBLEM

Have you ever heard someone say this about a player? "She has some power." "She has a pretty swing." "But she's inconsistent against good pitching." You know exactly who I'm talking about. The cage star. The BP legend. The player who crushes when balls are tossed right down the middle, and struggles when competition starts. Why does this happen?

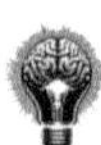

We're measuring outcomes in ideal environments and expecting those numbers to translate to competitive environments. Think about what we measure: The Body (Kinematic sequence, Angular velocity of each rotational axis, Ground forces), The Bat (Attack angle, Bat speed), The Ball (Launch angle, Ball exit speed). These are all outcomes.

Identifying our on-field production is what's missing. Is it a swing or hitting issue?

The Truth

Those impressive numbers that show up when a ball is tossed right down the middle in the cage environment are likely to disappear in the competitive environment. It's like training for a boxing match by only hitting a stationary heavy bag. Sure, you'll develop power, but will you be able to land that punch when your opponent is moving, faking, and trying to knock your head off? The environment changes everything.

I've discovered one thing through years of trial and error: The more you verify, the less you will trust what "they" say and trust what you see. Here's the beautiful part: when you address the essentials–discipline, rhythm, timing, position, and path–these numbers will be close to where they should be anyway.

 You're working backward. You're trying to fix the numbers hoping the hitting improves. Elite coaches fix the hitting, knowing the numbers will follow.

CHALLENGE #1: THE CAGE REALITY CHECK

For your next three cage sessions, do this experiment:

SESSION 1: Down-the-Middle Data - Take 20 swings on balls tossed perfectly down the middle. Record your best exit velocity. Note your "best" numbers.

SESSION 2: Competition Simulation - Take 20 swings on varied speeds and locations (simulate game conditions). Record your exit velocity. Note your average numbers.

SESSION 3: The Comparison - Calculate the difference between your "best" and "average." Write down what changed (timing? position? path?). Ask yourself: Which environment better prepares me for Friday night?

Before you run this challenge, you need to understand something critical about how to actually use data...

APPLES TO APPLES, NOT APPLES TO ORANGES

THE DATA CHECKLISTS

Let me give you the framework for when data can be useful. Pay close attention, because if you use it wrong, you'll make things worse.

Mechanics Testing:

Load (The initial move that precedes the kinematic sequence, putting you in position to create stretch and maximize power. Based on your movement type, leg kick, toe tap, heel up/heel down, open to close, test and compare body, ball, or bat measurements to determine what works best to improve the numbers).

Shift (Following the load, this occurs in most athletes. For those who load up and stay back, test both positions: staying over the rear leg versus a small weight shift forward).

Degrees of Rotation (All players don't have the same finish. Test balls down the middle with the back shoulder pointing closer to the pitcher, compared to finishing with the chest square to the pitcher).

Finish Type (Should you finish with one or two hands? Ball data and bat path would be great assessments).

Hitting – Pitch Types Testing:

In and Out (Monitor timing and contact points to identify desired proximity to your body. Let the ball get closer, and try some further out front).

Up and Down (Assess the path of the bat coming through the zone).

Adjustability (Throw a variety of speeds and locations to identify distinct differences between feel-good tosses and tosses with variability).

Rhythm (Test a quick rhythm against a slow rhythm).

The Problem

You're comparing apples to oranges. When game planning or establishing an approach, consider two types of programs: KNOWN REPS (Coaches who give you variability reps and those who give you known reps of speed and location). If data is going to be used in a "known reps" system, you should be hunting speed and location in the game! Shouldn't you consider eliminating the use of data where reps are random?

You could find yourself comparing apples to oranges if your testing environment doesn't pair with your performance environment.

The Truth

Think of it like this: imagine you're training to be a chef. Choose option A or B.

Option A: Practice making the perfect omelet every single day. Master one dish. Get really good at that one thing. Then measure your speed, consistency, and quality on that one dish.

Option B: Practice making different dishes every day under time pressure, with missing ingredients, using different equipment. Never know what you're making until the order comes in.

Which option prepares you for a real restaurant kitchen? Neither is wrong. However, your practice environment must match your performance environment.

Known Reps Method: Best for teams that prepare hitters for the expected game planning. When pitcher profiles simulate the speed and location of whom you'll face in the circle. The data collection of the known, paired with disciplined hitters on time and on path, will likely give the body and ball the same performance in both environments.

Variability Reps Method: When your program promotes adjustability or a "see it and hit it" philosophy, eliminate the data collection when the machine is set up right down the middle or in a known speed and location. Remember: compare apples to apples, not fruit to fruit. Variability reps are essential for adjusting your approach in all 0-2 strike counts. So, consider this: Would you go to the gym and perform only curls, deadlifts, bench press, and squats to

prepare for a CrossFit competition based on your data collected in the gym? Probably not.

There's a deeper issue we need to address, one that most completely miss...

THE ROOT CAUSE

THE MEDICAL OFFICE METAPHOR

Imagine you walk into a medical care facility. Everyone in the waiting room is coughing. What's the first thing the physician does when you get called back? Do they immediately prescribe cough medicine? No. They perform a series of diagnostic steps: Ask questions to determine your symptoms, inquire about your environment (Where have you been? Who have you been around?), check vitals (blood pressure, temperature), examine (look at your throat, in your ears), test (swab or blood sample).

Why? Because the common cold, COVID, influenza, and sinus infections can all present with a cough (outcome). The physician doesn't treat the symptom (cough). The physician treats the cause (infection). Better yet, depending on the problem, the physician will refer you to a specialist when symptoms don't subside.

The Problem

Most players experience fruit treatment (symptoms) over root treatment (cause). Let me give you a real example.

The Brooke Story

Greg brought his daughter Brooke in for a tune-up after a tournament full of inconsistency. "They say she's pulling off the ball," Greg said. "How do they know that?" I asked. Then I presented this question: "If the pulling-off position was present on an inside pitch resulting in a double down the line, compared to a pitch on the outer part of the plate, is that pulling off or timing?" "Great question," he replied.

When Brooke arrived, I asked what her challenges were. She told me she was pulling off. Then I asked about her ball flight. This is where it gets interesting.

THE ASSESSMENT QUESTIONS

Before I can diagnose the root cause, I need to ask the right questions. Not about the swing, but the competitive environment. Alternative Format (Checklist Style):

Alternative Format (Checklist Style):

Answering no to question 1 or 2, eliminates the need to answer the others.

1. Did you have a plan: ☐ Yes ☐ No

2. You stick to the plan: ☐ Yes ☐ No*Answer no to 1 or 2 stop here.

3. Pitch position: ☐ Up ☐ Down

4. How did you miss up: ☐ Over ☐ Under

5. Timing: ☐ Early ☐ Late

These questions reveal the root. Now here are the most important questions that nobody asks:

The Truth

THE MOST CRITICAL DATA POINTS: Did you monitor where the catcher received most of the pitches, in or out? Did you work on your rhythm and timing during your time in the dugout? If you have access, did you simulate the speed and/or location of the pitches you knew were going to be thrown by the pitcher?

Here's the brutal truth: What good is the kinematic sequence, angular velocities, and ball exit speed if you cannot identify the source of your contact problems? In most cases, it has nothing to do with the body. It has everything to do with your mind and how you use it.

Until I feel comfortable with you and ensure we're speaking the same language, I cannot trust verbal assessments. Not yours, not your parents', not your coach's. The outcome data is directly associated with the input data: How did you miss - over or under?

How was your timing - early or late? Did you miss across on a drop ball down and in? Discipline or not?

The fruit production is primarily based on the environment where the tree is planted and the uptake of nutrients in that environment. You're trying to change the fruit without examining the soil.

CHALLENGE #2: THE ROOT CAUSE AUDIT

After your next competitive at-bat where you struggle, answer these questions HONESTLY:

INPUT DATA (What you controlled): Did you have a plan before the at-bat? Were you disciplined to the plan? Did you monitor where the catcher was setting up? Did you work your rhythm in the dugout? Did you simulate any pitches during your preparation? Did you visualize your bat position and path?

OUTPUT DATA (What happened): How did you miss - over or under? How was your timing - early or late? What was the ball flight?

Now answer this: Was your struggle a body problem or a mind problem? Be honest. You can't fix what you won't acknowledge. This gets even more interesting...

KEEPING IT SIMPLE

THE QUALITY AT-BAT STANDARD

Give me the player who, after all development is complete, faces live pitching and consistently: Makes great decisions, sticks to the plan, Swings with intent, has adjustability in your swing. I think we call those quality at-bats producers.

Here's my quality at-bat checklist. Notice what's NOT on it:

SWING RX QUALITY AT-BATS

Date: ________   Opponent: ________   At-Bat #: ______

#	Quality At-Bat Criteria	Yes	No	Notes
1	Did you have a plan?	☐	☐	
2	Were you disciplined?	☐	☐	
3	Were you on time?	☐	☐	
4	Did you swing with intent?	☐	☐	
5	Did you identify your miss type?	☐	☐	
6	Did you adjust your next AB?	☐	☐	
7	Did you adjust on your next pitch, if the same?	☐	☐	
8	If no movement adjustment, was compensation applied?	☐	☐	

Quality At-Bat Score: _______ / 8

Do you see kinematic sequence on that list? Do you see the launch angle? Do you see exit velocity? No. Because those are outputs of a good process.

The Problem

When you made the initial investment in fancy devices, be honest: Who were they for? Were they for the athlete? Or were they for you? Were they used to entertain or educate? Look, I get it. These players have dreams. In the pursuit of dreams, there's a lot of money and time either invested or mostly spent to achieve those dreams.

The Truth

Being right for one player to enhance their career and then forcing that same drill on another player could absolutely destroy their career.

> Oftentimes, these fancy devices are used to impress instead of improving.

As it relates to data today and the problems my players have, I've reached this conclusion:

> Until we have adequately found consistency in the general areas of the strike zone, learned to sit on fast or slow speed, and learned to adjust to previous misses... the phone is enough data for me right now.

Think about what you can see when video is slowed down: you can identify if the player's torso is in the proper position to produce the ideal path. You can assess the adequacy of the attack angle when the bat is incoming to the ball. You can see the ball flight after contact. Better instructors and coaches don't need launch angle information; they can see it.

When you keep it simple, you maximize the efficiency of your time in the cage to address the essential needs of the player. There are exceptions—players can use these tools for buy-in—but in truth, they don't provide solutions.

THE DEVICE VS. EYES COMPARISON

Think of data devices like GPS navigation: GPS is incredibly helpful when you're driving to an unfamiliar location. It gives you turn-by-turn directions, traffic updates, alternative routes. What if you're trying to teach someone to drive? Would you tell them: "Just follow the GPS"?

Or would you teach them to: watch the road, check their mirrors, Feel the car's response, anticipate other drivers, read traffic patterns? The GPS is a tool. It's not a substitute for driving skill.

Data devices are the same. They're tools that can confirm what you're seeing or quantify improvement. They're not a substitute for coaching skill, the ability to identify root causes and address them.

You may find your eye can be the best tool when you know what to look for.

THE USE OF THE EYES (What's demonstrated) AND THE PHONE (Discussing it)

On this particular tournament day in Oxford, MS, we were facing a team from Missouri. Up comes Lauren, who I didn't know at the time. The first pitch she swung at was a swing and miss. One of the most efficient and explosive swings to this day. Considering she had a quick tempo and early timing, she was the perfect candidate for a change up. I called the pitch and held my breath each time the ball was released from the pitcher's hand. Lauren ended the game 0-3! I approached her and said, "Don't get down on yourself, you have a great swing."

Lauren responded immediately, "Get away from me, you kept throwing me those change ups." "Well, you kept swinging at them", I said. There we were, two strangers, talking like we had known each other for years.

The first remote hitting session, no video

On my two-hour ride home, I ended up talking to Lauren and her mother about what I saw, and why we refused to throw her specific pitches. I described her timing vulnerabilities, which indicated what pitch to call. Since I would never face her again, I shared with her the risk of treating all strikes the same. Followed with considerations to hunt speed and location to get the most out of her powerful swing.

When the call ended, Lauren said she just had the best hitting lesson ever without stepping foot in the cage. I ended the call by challenging her to have discipline rounds in the cage and monitor her hard contact. A few weeks later, Lauren notified me with great excitement. She faced a pitcher throwing a change up, she hunted it and smoked it!

CHALLENGE #3: THE ONE-WEEK SIMPLE APPROACH

For the next week, eliminate ALL data devices from your cage sessions. Just bring: Your phone (for video), Your eyes, Your mind. Focus ONLY on: Bat path through the zone and ball flight after contact. After each session, review slow-motion video and answer: Was the torso in position? Was the path appropriate for the pitch location? What does ball flight tell me about timing and contact?

At the end of the week, ask yourself: Did I lose anything by eliminating the devices? Or did I gain clarity?

The Data Decision

PATH ONE: The Data-Driven Approach - Invest in technology. Track every metric. Compare numbers constantly. Hope improvement in numbers translates to performance.

PATH TWO: The Clarity-Driven Approach - Use your eyes to identify root causes. Address obvious problems first. Use data to confirm, not discover. Focus on process, trust outputs will follow.

Neither path is completely wrong. Although one path has a much higher risk of: creating cage stars who crumble in competition, missing obvious problems while chasing perfect numbers, Overwhelming players with information overload, and losing efficiency in your limited cage time.

The Final Question

Let me ask you something that will reveal which path you're actually on: In your last ten cage sessions, how much time did you spend: A) Setting up equipment, calibrating devices, downloading data, and discussing numbers? B) Actually, watching the player move, identifying root causes, and making adjustments?

Be honest. Your answer reveals whether you're coaching the player or the data.

The 90/10 Principle (Revisited)

Remember this from Chapter 3? 90% = Your Mind, 10% = Your Body. Here's how it applies to data: 90% of improvement comes from addressing decision and discipline. Unfortunately, some coaches spend 90% of their time outside of the 90%. Elite coaches flip that script. They use their eyes, and their mind to address the 90%. Then, if needed, they bring in data to optimize the final 10%.

The Brooke Conclusion

Remember Brooke from earlier? The player who was "pulling off"? After asking my assessment questions and watching her on video, here's what I discovered: The problem wasn't pulling off. The problem was late timing on inside pitches (that was actually survival mode). We didn't need kinematic sequence data. We didn't need launch angle measurements. We didn't need exit velocity reports. We needed to address her rhythm, timing, and plan.

Once we did, her "pulling off" problem disappeared. Well she actually wasn't pulling off, she was just early. The fruit (symptom) changed because we addressed the root (issue).

Your Choice

You now have a decision to make. Will you continue chasing impressive numbers in ideal environments? Or will you pursue impressive performance in competitive environments? Will you use data to impress? Or will you use clarity to improve?

The choice defines whether you become a cage star or a game changer. Here's what you need to know: the players who learn to be right in competition, not just right in the cage, are the ones who fulfill dreams like Lana's. They're the ones holding posters at age ten and playing in championship games at age nineteen. They're not the ones with the best kinematic sequence. They're the ones who addressed the main thing: becoming undeniable in competition.

FINAL CHALLENGE: THE 30-DAY DATA FAST

For 30 days no ball exit speed measurements, no launch angle data, no kinematic sequence reports. Just your phone video, your eyes, root cause identification, Process focus.

Track these instead: quality at-bats in competition, Ability to adjust between at-bats, Consistency against varied speeds/locations, Confidence growth.

At the end of 30 days, answer honestly: Did your competitive performance improve or decline? That answer will tell you everything you need to know about the role of data in your development.

You now understand that fancy data isn't the answer. Your phone captures more *useful* information than most $10,000 systems. Addressing the obvious beats measuring meaningless outcomes that don't provide solutions to your swing or hitting problems.

Here's the problem: even with the right data approach, even with simplified assessment methods, even with your phone instead of expensive technology... you still don't know what you're actually looking for.

Think about it: what good is having assessment tools if you don't know what a "good" assessment reveals? What's the point of simplifying data collection if you can't interpret what the data means? You're a doctor with a stethoscope and no medical training. You can hear the heartbeat, yet you don't know if it's healthy or dangerous.

Right now, you probably think you know your strengths and weaknesses. You've heard coaches tell you what you do well. You've felt successful on certain pitches. You have vague ideas about your "hot zones." Here's the brutal truth: you could be wrong about all of it.

In the next chapter, you're going to discover the assessment system that reveals your actual strengths and vulnerabilities, not what you think they are, not what you hope they are, but what they really are. You're going to learn why the best players in the nation at elite camps already know their holes. You're going to face uncomfortable truths about yourself that you've been avoiding.

The players who face these truths break through. The players who avoid them plateau. The question is: are you brave enough to discover who you really are as a hitter?

FINDING YOUR STRENGTHS AND VULNERABILITIES

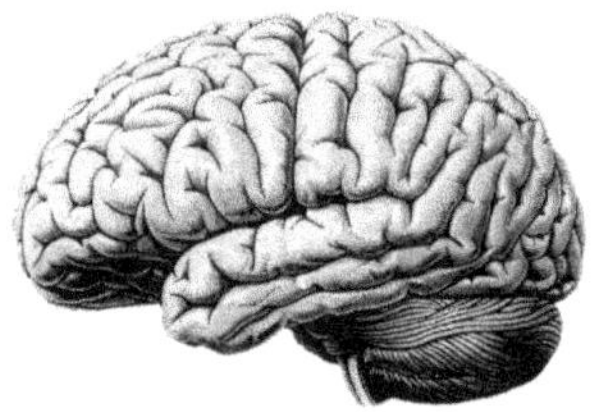

The Assessment Rx

"You can't fix what you won't face. You can't grow from what you refuse to measure." - Coaching Wisdom

THE PHONE CALL NOT RECEIVED

Your season's not going the way you planned. The college coaches who you thought would be interested, never reached out. The at-bats that used to feel easy? They feel like you're swinging underwater. The pitches you used to crush? They're now finding leather instead of grass. So you pick up the phone.

Traditionally, when my phone rings, it's a player who is no longer having the same success. They've discovered their future playing goals may be at risk. Maybe they are realizing that baseball and softball careers are more like timers and less like a clock: A time for exposure and a time for production. The problem. Players understand the clock, not the timer. There is still playing time remaining on the clock, however the time to develop has run out, or is running out.

It's about building on your strengths and reducing your areas of vulnerability now. The problem is most players have no idea what their actual strengths are. They think they know. They don't.

> What you don't know about yourself will absolutely destroy you in competition.

At a minimum you should understand what you do well.

THE GEORGIA SOFTBALL CAMP DISCOVERY

THE CAGE THAT REVEALED EVERYTHING

A few years ago, I was working at a camp at the University of Georgia. A great opportunity to work with future college players that possess high-level talent. I was stationed in one of the cages, ready to throw. Two players walked in, I started their rounds with pitches right down the middle. This gave me the opportunity to monitor their natural bat path, where the barrel wanted to go without any manipulation.

After observing their tendencies, I did something intentional. I threw pitches directly at the holes in their swings, placing them away from the sweet spot and closer to the handle.

The Problem

Here's what most players don't understand: you don't know your swing as well as you think you do. You know what feels comfortable. You know what pitches you like to see. You know what you hit hard when everything's perfect. You have no idea what your actual vulnerabilities are.

Think about it: when was the last time you systematically tested yourself on? Inside vs. outside pitches? Up vs. down locations? Fast vs. slow speeds in each zone? Your ability to hit your "weak" zones? If you're like most players, the answer is never.

You take your swings down the middle. You feel good. You assume you're ready for Friday night. Then Friday night comes and the pitcher lives on the edges. Leaving you helpless.

The Truth

What I discovered at the Georgia camp changed how I assess every player who walks into my cage. The best players at the camp didn't have answers for each area of the strike zone. They had one thing: discipline. They didn't swing at pitches in the cage they knew they couldn't square up.

The LSU softball camp was no different! To ensure this wasn't a coincidence, I used the same technique at an LSU camp the following year. I got the same result.

> The elite players knew their limitations. They understood their zones of strength and zones of vulnerability. They had the discipline not to chase pitches they couldn't handle.

The average players? They swung at everything labeled "strike" and wondered why they struggled against good pitching.

THE BETH TORINA OFF-SPEED DROP I WASN'T HUNTING

The Setup You Don't See Coming

At the end of the LSU camp, I was standing next to Rock Thompson, watching the final rounds wrap up. Players were packing up, and parents were loading cars. Another successful camp in the books. Coach Beth Torina walks up and asks, "Rogerick, who are your top three?" This wasn't a question I expected. I wasn't expecting to be scouted while I was scouting. This was like the off-speed drop I wasn't hunting. I had about three seconds to not look like an idiot in front of the coach.

The Decision

I looked up to the stands and pointed. "I can't remember their names," I admitted. "The red and black jersey right there. The white and blue jersey right there. And the grey jersey there." She paused, looking where I pointed, then back at me. "Okay. Those are players on the radar." She walked away. I exhaled.

The Validation

An elite coach asked me to identify elite talent in about three seconds, based on what I'd observed during camp. **No Data**. No stats. No recruiting profiles. No prior knowledge.

The three I picked were already on LSU's radar.

Why It Matters

You know what Coach Torina wasn't asking me? "Who has the prettiest swing?" "Who hit the ball the hardest?" "Who has the best mechanics?" She was asked, "Who do you think can hit?"

Here's what separated those three players from everyone else at that camp:

The Three Elements:

DECISION-MAKING (They made great decisions in their rounds. They didn't swing at everything. They hunted their zones. They had discipline).

NATURAL MOVEMENT (Their swings weren't perfect, but they were efficient for the way their bodies moved. They moved well naturally. No robotic positions. Just athleticism).

LOW VULNERABILITY (They had damage zones they dominated and weak zones they protected. Their holes were small or well-compensated).

The Uncomfortable Truth

You are always being judged on how many things you do well, not how perfect one thing is. The young ladies who captured my attention, and Coach Torina's attention, weren't the ones with the prettiest swings or the most launch monitor data. They were the ones who understood themselves well enough to make good decisions, move efficiently, and minimize their vulnerabilities.

The Question You Need to Ask

If a college coach walked up to your instructor right now and asked, "Who are your top three?" If he or she is honest, would you be one of them?

HONESTY MOMENT

If a college coach asked YOUR coach to name their top three, would you make the list?

☐ Yes, I make great decisions and have low vulnerability

☐ Maybe, I'm talented but still inconsistent

☐ No, I'm still working on understanding myself

☐ Not sure, I don't know what my coach thinks

If you answered anything other than YES, you have work to do. That work starts with the assessments in this chapter.

The Takeaway

Being put on the spot by Beth Torina taught me something critical. Elite coaches can spot elite hitters in minutes. It's not the mechanics; it's their decision-making, movement efficiency and low vulnerability. You either have it, or you don't. If you don't have it yet, this chapter will help you build it. What is your answer when the opposition finds your vulnerable area?

VIRGINIA AND THE VULNERABILITY DISCOVERY

YOU SAW IT, BUT JUST DIDN'T PAY ATTENTION - 2024 WCWS Regionals

During the road to the Women's College World Series, the score of the Virginia game was announced. They had just defeated the nation's leading home run team twice. The leading home run team was scoreless against them in two games. "What?!", I thought. I immediately placed my phone in front of the television and recorded every pitch thrown by Virginia during the on-demand game.

There it was! The same swings and the same pitch locations for both games. Up and in with velocity. Down and away with off-speed. It was nothing fancy, it was clear Coach Jamie saw some similarities throughout the line up. She didn't get fancy. She stayed consistent.

Coach Jamie later confirmed the game plan was a combination of scouting hitters and reviewing the data. Jamie had her pitcher prepared to hunt and the batters were prey. Just know, your vulnerabilities will be pursued! Therefore, you would assume the opposite of your vulnerable zone is your good pitch zone.

WHAT IS A "GOOD PITCH"?

THE INTERVIEW CLICHÉ

You hear it interview after interview: "Find a good pitch to hit." Walk through any ballpark and listen carefully. Coaches yelling from the dugout: "Find a good pitch to hit!" Parents from the stands: "Wait for your pitch!"

The Problem

Most players have no idea what a good pitch actually is. Try this experiment. Ask a player, "What pitches should you swing at with less than two strikes?" Most will tell you: "A strike." Now ask yourself, "What location in the strike zone do you NOT want with the game on the line, last inning, down by one run, 3-2 count?"

Players will tell you what pitch they don't want with the game on the line. They'll also tell you they'll swing at any strike with less than two strikes. Try This: In case you missed that nugget. Ask a player what pitch they don't want, bottom of the last inning. Runner on second, and their team is down by 1. Most players know their vulnerability. We are just not having discussions with them.

Do you see the problem? Imagine you're playing poker. Someone asks you, "What's a good hand?" You answer: "Any face card." That's not a strategy. That's desperation. A good hand depends on: what you're holding, what's on the table, what your opponent likely has, what stage of the game you're in. A "good pitch" works the same way.

The Pitch Confusion

Let me give you a specific example that may expose the flaw in your thinking. If a pitcher throws both a drop ball at 65 mph and a curveball at 65 mph in the same location, which one is your pitch? Most players would say: "Whichever one I recognize." Wrong answer. The real question isn't, what is your pitch? The real question is, what is your timing and spot?

If both pitches are 65 mph in the same location, they require the same timing, same body position, and same barrel position. I understand the phrase "find a good pitch to hit." However, I'm not sure players understand it as well as they hear it. In order for you to commit to a good pitch in competition, there should be clarity and understanding in the cage before competition.

The Truth

Here's the definition that changes everything:

SWING RX DEFINITION OF A GOOD PITCH WHEN HUNTING LESS THAN TWO STRIKES: A speed and location you are looking for, are in rhythm for, and are on time for.

It's just that simple. Not "a strike." Not "something over the plate." Not "a pitch I like." A speed and location you can time and destroy. How do you discover what that is?

When these three elements are paired up, you have a great opportunity for hard contact!

THE ASSESSMENT PROCESS

THE 50-PITCH TEST

Here's how you discover your actual strengths and vulnerabilities, not what you think they are.

SETUP REQUIREMENTS: First, you need the ability to front-toss into each corner of the strike zone. Second, the ability to observe ball flights that would travel at or slightly over the infielders' heads. This eliminates the need for expensive equipment to capture data. Optionally, you may use a radar gun to measure ball exit speed. If you've seen enough bat-to-ball contact and are familiar with the player, you can grade contact to any level you desire.

Trust me: I've had several college players in my cage, and I selectively take out the radar gun. It doesn't take a trained eye to know when a ball is squared up and hit back on the same line it came in from. In addition, they know it also!

THE PROTOCOL: Start by throwing 10 pitches in each area of the strike zone (up-in, up-away, down-in, and down-away). Then throw 10 pitches right down the middle. Total: 50 pitches. Grade each pitch by the type of contact and path. At the end of each area, you should have a great idea of where the barrel naturally comes through the zone.

The Problem

Most players never test themselves this way. Why? They just don't know! It's easier to believe you "can hit anything" than to face concrete evidence that you have massive holes in specific zones. Think about it: when you go to the cage, what do you do? Take BP down the middle, hit a few to feel good, Maybe work on "mechanics," Leave feeling confident. You never intentionally throw at your weaknesses. You never systematically test each zone. You never create a heat map of your actual performance. You're practicing in the dark, hoping the lights turn on during the game.

The Truth

Why is this 50-pitch test so valuable? For players you have difficulty breaking through to, you now have concrete evidence of what you don't do well. Not opinion. Not feeling. Practical Data. For players hungry to get better, the data combined with video shows which areas of the zone you may need at the beginning of an improvement plan. In a team environment this information can be used for putting together the best lineup. Great coaches understand matchups. If a pitcher dominates down in the zone and your best hitter performs best up in the zone, do you adjust the lineup?

You may use these same methods if you have tools that will capture ball flight and bat data. You need honesty and a system.

Understanding The Data

Here's something critical: this data collection does not provide answers for swing issues. These are only outcomes. However, the data can assist in further defining what a good pitch is. Today's pitcher's fastball you love in zone nine could be tomorrow's pitcher's curveball. Both are the same if they're the same speed and location. Same timing, body position, barrel position, right?

The same location and speed of a different pitch have a greater opportunity of finding the barrel than a fastball at 67 mph versus a fastball at 57 mph. Speed and locations that pair up well with your timing is where you are finding your consistency.

CHALLENGE #1: THE 50-PITCH TRUTH TEST

This week, run the 50-pitch assessment:

Grading Scale Considerations:

A: Line drive and hard one hop ground balls.

C: Hard multiple hop ground balls.

F: Pop ups, soft ground balls, fouls and misses

Table 5.0 - Zone Contact Grading Scale

Round	Zone	Pitches	Purpose	Grading
1	Up-In	10	Assess contact & barrel path	A = 5 C = 2 F = 0
2	Up-Away	10	Test opposite high zone	A = 5 C = 2 F = 0
3	Mid-In	10	Measure reaction speed	A = 5 C = 2 F = 0

4	Mid-Away	10	Gauge adjustability	A = 5 C = 2 F = 0
5	Middle	10	Benchmark	A = 5 C = 2 F = 0

Calculate your score for each zone. Which zone was your highest score? Which zone was your lowest score? Did the results match what you THOUGHT your strengths were? Would you have swung at all those pitches in a game?

Write down your answers. The reason is you can't improve what you won't acknowledge. The real test isn't in the cage...

BECOMING A REAL HITTING COACH (BY LEARNING TO READ HITTERS)

The Pitch Calling Education

About seven years ago, I was coaching with Motion 02. My responsibility was to put hitters in position to improve their offensive production and exposure before college coaches. During games, I would sit next to Rodney, who called pitches at the time. I started doing something different. I would read tempo, body position, bat position, bat path, foul ball flights, take reactions to balls or strikes.

I started to see how those elements would produce a path that favored the hitter, and how to suggest a pitch that would go further from the barrel and closer to the hole in their swing. I would often ask Rodney, "What pitch are you thinking right here?" If his answer was a pitch that would fit their bat path and timing, I would suggest something different. That turned into a great partnership. Then came the ultimate test...

The Prospects Game

One particular day, we were facing the Prospects, picked to be the best team in our pool. After the umpire said, "Play ball," Rodney turned to me and asked, "Would you like to call pitches?" My first thought, why this team? The best team we've played since I joined the coaching staff. Not to mention, they were coached by a former Power 5 player and a travel ball coach/dad who had a ton of experience. Then I remembered something critical.

The Problem

Most hitters have the same problems because they're taught the same things. Think about your own training: "Swing at strikes," "Be aggressive," "Get a good pitch to hit," "Stay short to the ball," "Drive the ball up the middle." Everyone hears the same cues. Everyone develops similar tendencies. Everyone has predictable holes. If you know what to look for, hitters will tell you exactly what or where not to throw.

The Truth: The Checkers Strategy

I used simple logic. First, I tested the players with pitches Belle could locate well. She only had three primary pitches: fastball, curve, and screw. One was added during that game, a straight fastball. Considering players are often told to "swing at strikes," I could quickly determine where their timing or tendencies were.

We started off with pitches she would locate very well for a ball. Yes. I intentionally threw balls to some hitters. The areas where hard takes were made. This would give me an idea of where their attention may have been.

I looked for timing of the front foot, stride tempo, spine position, how the barrel came through the zone on foul balls. These indicators would provide me information for intentional strikes and balls. For strikes, I would throw away from the areas of the hitter's timing, and the areas where the spine would produce the best path.

Belle located her pitches well and made sure we missed closer to the handle of the bat instead of the barrel. Think of it like boxing. You don't need to knock someone out. You just need to make them miss and tire them out while they swing at air.

The Adjustment

After the third inning, their coach huddled the team up and aggressively got on the players. I had no idea what went on in that huddle. Considering that staff's experience, I assumed she told the players to make an adjustment. That was the only logical thing to do since I was beating them with the same pitch, fastball and screw.

Their next at-bat, I made a simple adjustment. I just went further in. Since they tried to get off the plate to hit what we were throwing, I moved the plate right along with them. That wasn't even the best part. Now I could go to Belle's best pitch for a strike with more of the plate, curveball outside to righties.

They were now taking those pitches with less than two strikes or flailing at them for weak grounders with two strikes. It's great to get in a hitter's head. The goal is to read hitters, create failure, and get the coach in the hitter's head right along with them. This strategy was a simple checkers move.

The Result

The game ended in a 0-0 tie. Belle threw 55 pitches in five innings. No walks. One strikeout. One hit. That one hit. On me. I didn't reposition the shortstop after shifting her on the previous batter. Players with a "swing" plan are no match for a pitcher with a "pitch" plan. Just like every batter can swing and not hit. Every player on the mound or in the circle can throw, though not pitch.

As a hitter, you are no match for a pitcher who can locate, and a coach who knows your swing better than you know it. Your swing will tell a pitching coach exactly what they want. If they just pay attention. How do you actually read hitters in real time?

READING THE HITTER: THE TELLS

The Poker Analogy

In poker, a "tell" is an unconscious behavior that reveals information about a player's hand. Good poker players don't focus on the cards; they focus on the tells. Hitting works the same way. Every hitter has tells that reveal their timing, their barrel path, their vulnerabilities. You just need to know what to look for.

The Hitting Tells:

LATE TIMING → Inside with a fastball (Front foot late to land, Rushed swing, Bat dragging behind body).

EARLY TIMING → Outside curve or change (Front foot early to land, Barrel dumps early, Pull-side foul balls).

TORSO/SPINE ANGLED TO CATCHER → Up and in with fastball (Weight stuck on back leg, Hands drop to get under ball, Can't get in line at this location).

LOOPY BAT PATH → Up and in (Barrel takes long route to ball, Drops below ball before contact, Vulnerable to elevation).

DOWN BAT PATH → Down and in (Barrel comes from above ball, Chops down on contact, Vulnerable to pitches down).

The Problem

You're being read right now. Every at-bat. Every pitch. Every foul ball. Good pitching coaches are sitting in the dugout charting: Where you foul balls off, What pitches you take, What pitches you swing through, How your body moves in the box.

The Alternative: Can't read the body or bat, read the foul ball:

Straight back - under miss → Go further up.

Straight back - over miss → Go further down.

Pull side fouls → Slower away.

Opposite field fouls → Faster in.

Don't mix up the pitches with biased pitch calling. Match up the pitching based on what the swing is calling.

Please forgive me! I just told throwing coaches how to pitch! They're building a profile. A scouting report. A blueprint for how to beat you. And you have no idea it's happening. You think you're just "struggling" or "in a slump." The truth is simpler and more brutal: You're being systematically exploited.

The Truth

The elite hitters understand something that average hitters miss: You need to become harder to read. This means: Minimizing your tells, understanding your own tendencies, making adjustments between at-bats, forcing pitchers to rely on their defense and not your weaknesses. Think of it like chess. Beginners play one move at a time. Masters think three moves ahead. Beginners react to what's thrown. Masters dictate what's thrown.

CHALLENGE #2: THE SELF-SCOUTING REPORT

For your next three games, become your own scout:

After each at-bat, answer: What was my timing - early, late, or on time? Where did I foul balls off (pull side, middle, opposite field)? What pitches did I take that were strikes? What did my body position reveal about my timing? If I was the pitcher, what would I throw next time?

After the game, answer: Did I make any adjustments? Did the pitcher identify my holes? Did they exploit them? What would I do differently next game?

Be brutally honest, as the pitcher will be. There's one more layer to this that changes everything...

THE LSU CAMP REVELATION

THE TALENT PARADOX

Let me tell you about a second camp experience at LSU. Once again, some of the best talent in the nation. This time, I was working on a pitching machine lane with Taylor, that gave players a variety of pitch types. Some of the holes were obvious. When an opportunity presented itself, I inquired about those vulnerable areas. To no surprise, the elite prospects knew where their challenges were. These were some of the most talented players in the nation, future D1 stars, who knew exactly what they couldn't hit.

The Problem

The most talented players will be granted opportunities while the least talented will be limited. What if the less talented had the skills to adjust their approaches. Maybe they would be considered a part of the elite. This is even more profound in this transfer portal era. You could be in the process of developing, while someone else comes in developed and ready!

Think about that. If you're less talented, you have less margin for error. You get fewer at-bats to work through struggles. You face tougher competition with less rope from coaches. You can't afford to have holes in your swing. Here's the twist: the talented players at

LSU knew their holes. They could articulate them. They understood their vulnerabilities. They still got opportunities because their strengths were so dominant they could survive with weaknesses. You probably don't have that luxury.

The Truth

After my conversations with pitching coaches, I've realized that pitchers don't have to solve problems for batters. They only need to identify them. Fortunately for pitchers, they don't have to solve problems for batters, just identify them. That's the hitter's problem to deal with. Pitching coaches understand their task is to disrupt the rhythm and timing of the hitter. However, for whatever reason, most hitters have not discovered they should be attempting to accomplish the opposite of what the pitcher is trying to do.

Think about that paradox: Pitching coaches study hitters religiously. Hitters rarely study themselves. And the pitching coach knows you better than you know yourself or your hitting coach.

Challenge: Ask all coaches on your staff how they would pitch, to avoid your barrel. Then ask why. Unfortunately, you don't clearly understand yourself, nor do you understand the truth about velocity.

The Effective Velocity Layer

The task of hitting becomes even more intense when you're facing a pitcher who is effective velocity efficient. I'm not sure exactly how Perry Husband would describe it. I would say it's the combination of plus and minus speed by way of tunneling pitches, in addition to creating freezes and chases by batters. Pitchers who understand how to make you late or early and over or under based on location, speed and sequencing are playing chess, while you're playing checkers.

The Mirror Test

Let me ask you a question that will reveal everything about your approach to hitting: Do you spend more time studying pitchers or studying yourself? Be honest. Most hitters spend hours watching video of pitchers: What do they throw? How hard? What locations? What sequences?

They spend zero hours honestly assessing: What can I actually hit hard? What are my real vulnerabilities? How do I reveal my timing? What would I throw myself? You're trying to win a war without knowing your own weaknesses.

Honesty Moment: How often have you received a scouting report, of yourself?

CHALLENGE #3: THE VULNERABILITY AUDIT

This is the hardest challenge in this chapter because it requires complete honesty.

PART 1: IDENTIFY YOUR HOLES - Answer these questions: What location do you struggle with most? (Be specific: up-in, down-away, etc.) What speed gives you the most trouble? What pitch type do you struggle to identify? What's your most common miss direction? What do opposing coaches likely have in your scouting report?

PART 2: TEST YOUR HOLES - In your next three cage sessions: Spend 70% of your time working on your WEAKEST zone (applying corrective or compensation). Only 30% working on your strengths. Track your improvement in the weak zone.

PART 3: GAME APPLICATION - In your next competitive at-bat: Assume the pitcher knows your holes. Have a plan if they attack your weakness. Be ready to hunt your strength if they give it to you.

At the end of this process, answer: Did knowing my vulnerabilities make me better prepared or more anxious? Your answer reveals whether you're ready for the next level.

THE INTENTIONAL SYSTEM

THE PHONE CALL REVISITED

Remember how this chapter started? With you making that phone call as things aren't going the way you planned? Players who breakthrough are willing to face uncomfortable truths about themselves. They don't want to just "hit better." They want to understand their actual strengths (not imagined ones), identify their real vulnerabilities (not excuses), build discipline around what they do well, reduce exposure to what they don't.

This is what I call an intentional system. It's not about: taking more swings, working harder, wanting it more. It's about: Strategic self-awareness, disciplined practice in your weaknesses, confident hunting of your strengths in competition.

The Problem

Most players operate on hope. I hope the pitcher throws you something you can hit. I hope you recognize it in time. I hope you make good contact. I hope it finds grass. Hope is not a strategy.

The Truth

The players who dominate at the next level operate on knowledge. Knowledge of what they do well, their vulnerabilities, how pitchers will attack them, and how to adjust. They've done the 50-pitch test. They've run the self-scouting reports. They've spent hours in their weak zones instead of their comfort zones.

They know themselves better than anyone else knows them. When they step in the box, they're not hoping. They're hunting.

The Two Types Of Hitters

TYPE 1: THE REACTIVE HITTER - Waits to see what the pitcher gives them. Adjusts after mistakes. Hopes for a "good pitch." Doesn't understand their own zones. Gets exploited by good pitching.

TYPE 2: THE STRATEGIC HITTER - Knows exactly what they do well. Understand their vulnerabilities. Has a plan before every pitch. Is tooled with compensations. Make adjustments proactively.

Which type are you? Don't answer quickly. Look at your actual results. Do pitchers consistently beat you the same way? Do you make the same mistakes repeatedly? Do you struggle against good pitching? Do you know what your "good pitch" actually is? Your answers reveal your type.

The Final Question

Am I willing to face uncomfortable truths about my hitting in order to become undeniable? That's what the assessment process requires. Facing data that might contradict what you believe about yourself. Spending time in zones that feel awful. Admitting you have holes that pitchers will exploit. It's uncomfortable yet necessary.

The players at Georgia and LSU who had discipline in their weak zones, may become stars. However, the players who kept swinging at everything labeled "strike"? They may plateau.

Belle's dominant performance against the Prospects? It happened because I read the hitters better than they read themselves. Will you learn to read yourself before someone else does?

YOUR NEXT MOVE

OPTION 1: IGNORE THIS CHAPTER - Keep taking BP down the middle. Keep hoping for "good pitches." Keep getting exploited by good pitching. Keep wondering why you plateau.

OPTION 2: ACKNOWLEDGE BUT DON'T ACT - Recognize you have holes. Feel bad about them. Tell yourself you'll work on them "eventually." Never actually do the assessment. Stay stuck.

OPTION 3: COMMIT TO THE SYSTEM - Run the 50-pitch test this week. Do the self-scouting report for three games. Complete the vulnerability audit. Spend 70% of practice time in weak zones. Become a strategic hitter.

You've just discovered your actual strengths and vulnerabilities. You've run the assessments. You've faced uncomfortable truths. You know exactly where you produce and where you struggle. Now what do you do about it?

Here's where most players make a catastrophic mistake. They discover a weakness and immediately try to fix it. They identify a vulnerability and assume the answer is mechanical correction. What if the weakness can't be fixed? What if you don't have time to fix it? What if fixing it breaks something else that's working?

Right now, there's a player reading this who discovered their down-and-in weakness in Chapter 5. That player is already planning to spend the next month in the cage fixing their path, adjusting their torso position, and changing their stance. Here's what they don't know: They might be about to destroy their career by trying to fix something that should be compensated for instead.

In the next chapter, you're going to learn the most important decision you'll make as a hitter. You'll learn when to fix versus when to compensate. You're going to discover why Aaron Judge might be compensating instead of correcting. Why Alana Johnson chose one path over the other. Why two college second basemen are sharing time on the bench is because they chose wrong.

This isn't about mechanics versus approach anymore. This is about understanding the windows of opportunity, the reality of time constraints, and the strategic decision that determines whether you correct your way to the bench or compensate your way to production. The players who understand this distinction thrive. The players who don't understand it waste entire off-seasons working on the wrong things. Which player will you be?

CHAPTER 6

MECHANICS, RHYTHM, TIMING, AND PATH

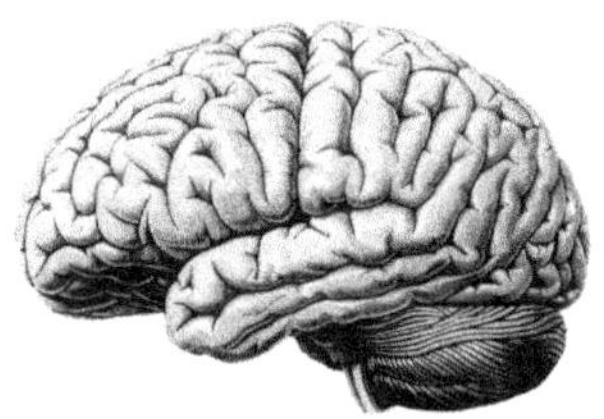

When to Fix, When to Compensate

"Your mechanics can adversely impact your timing, just as your timing can impact your mechanics. Hitting and mechanics work in tandem with one another." - Coaching Wisdom

MECHANICS MATTER, BUT THEY'RE NOT EVERYTHING

THE ACKNOWLEDGMENT

Let me be absolutely clear about something before we go any further: mechanics matter. I'm not anti-mechanics. I'm not telling you to ignore your swing. I'm not saying positions and movements are worthless.

What I am saying is this: the industry has convinced you that mechanics are the only thing that matters. That's the lie that's keeping talented players on the bench.

The Taylar Story

Let me tell you about Taylar. She came to me through a travel ball teammate. We'd meet near Memphis sometimes, other times Taylar and Shannon would drive almost three hours one way to work with me.

When we first got started, mechanics received 90% of our focus. Why? That's what we gurus do, right?

Taylar had two specific mechanical problems: She wasn't transferring her weight properly, and her torso position wasn't allowing her to create the best bat path at the top of the zone. These were real problems. Not imagined. Not philosophical. Real mechanical barriers that were limiting her production.

So, we addressed them. We did the work. We made the corrections.

The Problem

Taylar wasn't even the best player on her travel ball team. A player willing to drive three hours one way. Putting in the work and making corrections. She still wasn't the most talented but became one of the most talented.

How did she end up leading Itawamba Community College in home runs her freshman year after improving her stats significantly her senior year of high school?

The Truth

Once we addressed the mechanical barriers, we transitioned to the neck-up work. The approach. The game planning. The decision-making. The discipline. The timing. Hunting instead of reacting.

That's when Taylar separated herself.

Here's what most people miss: mechanics are the floor, not the ceiling.

> Mechanics give you the ability to hit the ball hard when you get your pitch. The mental game determines whether you recognize your pitch, whether you have the discipline to wait for it, whether you understand how to hunt it, and whether you can adjust when you don't get it.

Taylar's mechanical corrections gave her a foundation. Her mental development gave her production.

The Clarification

So let me be crystal clear about what this book is and isn't. This book is not anti-mechanics, telling you to ignore your swing, suggesting positions don't matter, or claiming you can think your way to good contact.

This book is revealing what's been invisible, exposing the 90% that gets 10% of the attention (sometimes 0%), showing you what happens after you've addressed mechanical barriers, and giving you the missing piece that separates talent from production.

The Reality Check

Think about your own development. Answer these questions honestly.

Mechanical focus: How many hours did you spent on swing work in the off season? How many drills have you done? How many videos have you analyzed? How much money have you spent on lessons?

Mental focus: How many hours have you spent on approach work? How many pitchers have you scouted? How many game plans have you created? How much time have you invested in understanding yourself as a hitter? How many solutions have you been given that are timing related? How much discipline work have you applied in the cage?

If the mechanical hours vastly outweigh the mental hours, you're training the 10% more than the 90%. This means you are not close to being the best version of yourself.

The Sequential Truth

Here's the framework that changes everything.

Phase 1: Mechanical Foundation (The 10%). Identify mechanical barriers, make necessary corrections, build a functional swing. Result: You CAN hit the ball hard.

Phase 2: Mental Development (The 90%). Understand your strengths and weaknesses, learn to game plan, develop a hunting mentality, build discipline to your approach.

Result: You DO hit the ball hard consistently.

Most players stop after Phase 1. They think the mechanical foundation is the finish line. It's not. It's the starting line.

Taylar understood this. She did the mechanical work. Then she did the mental work. That's why she led her team in home runs despite not being the most talented player on her high school travel ball team.

The Book's Focus

This book focuses on Phase 2 since that's what's been invisible. That's what's been ignored. That's what's been missing from nearly every batting cage in America.

Phase 1 matters, however everyone already knows Phase 1 exists. Every coach talks about mechanics. Every instructor teaches positions. Every clinic breaks down movements.

Who's teaching you to hunt instead of reacting? Who's teaching you to game plan like a college hitter? Who's teaching you to understand yourself well enough to articulate your strengths and weaknesses on Day 1 of college?

The 90% you've been missing, and that's what the rest of this chapter, and this book, is about.

The Bottom Line

Mechanics give you the ability to succeed. The mental game gives you the consistency to dominate. You need both. If you're spending 90% of your time on the 10%, you're preparing for the wrong test.

Taylar proved it. Madison Moak proved it. Lana Johnson proved it. Countless players I've worked with proved it.

Are you ready to train the 90% you've been missing? Mechanical corrections are the easy part. Every good instructor can help you with those. The mental game? That's where the separation happens. That's where we're going next.

The Subject That Gets All The Attention

Let's talk about the elephant in every batting cage across America, mechanics. Everyone obsesses over it. Coaches dissect it frame by frame. Parents pay thousands for instructors to "fix" it. Players spend hours drilling positions, angles, and movements. Come game time, you still have problems with a pitcher when you know what is coming.

Don't misunderstand me, mechanics matter. Especially at the start of playing the game. Here's what you need to understand before we go any further. Your mechanics can adversely impact your timing, just as your timing can impact your mechanics. Hitting and mechanics work in tandem with one another.

Think about the outcome you're actually trying to accomplish. What is a hitter trying to do? Hit the ball hard and get around the bases. It's just that simple. When you can put yourself in a position to hit the ball hard, it makes it tougher on the defense to make plays.

THE KYLE SCHWARBER TRUTH

THE DATA THAT CHANGES EVERYTHING

Let me show you something from Kyle Schwarber's 2025 data that will shift how you think about hitting.

When Schwarber hits the ball greater than 95 mph: batting average increases significantly, more extra-base hits, higher production overall.

When he hits the ball less than 85 mph: batting average plummets, weak contact, easy outs.

Table 6.0 - The Kyle Schwarber Truth

Kyle Schwarber Ball Exit Speed Velocity	Kyle Schwarber Ball Exit Speed Velocity	Kyle Schwarber Ball Exit Speed Velocity	Kyle Schwarber Ball Exit Speed Velocity
Zone	Location	Batting average. <85 mph ball exit speed	Batting average. > 95 mph ball exit speed
1	Up-Away	.333	.429
2	Up-Middle	.000	.643
3	Up-In	.571	.333
4	Mid-Away	.111	.405
5	Mid-Mid	.000	.509
6	Mid-In	.000	.417
7	Down-Away	.200	.188
8	Down-Middle	.000	.436
9	Down-In	1.000	.800

Mechanics alone will not allow you to achieve your desired outcome. If you don't believe me, the next time you talk to Kyle just ask him.

The Problem

You spend hours perfecting your hand position, elbow slot, hip-shoulder separation, back elbow angle, front knee position, and head stability.

Here's the brutal question: Does any of that matter if you're not hitting the ball hard consistently?

Imagine you're a race car driver obsessing over the angle of your steering wheel grip, the exact position of your feet on the pedals, and the posture of your spine in the seat. Meanwhile, your engine is underpowered, and your tires are bald.

All the perfect driving form in the world won't win the race if you can't generate speed and maintain control.

The Truth

Even the data supports the need for power and optimizing your production as a hitter. Your mechanics should serve one purpose - putting you in position to hit the ball hard.

If your "perfect mechanics" result in weak contact, they're not perfect, they're pretty. Guess what, pretty doesn't show up in box scores.

WHAT IS REQUIRED TO PRODUCE GREAT MECHANICS?

THE ROTATIONAL MOVER

First, it requires a great rotational mover, someone who, for their body type, can load, shift, generate stability, produce force, generate energy through rotation, and transfer and conserve that energy through the body to the baseball.

The Problem

Some will have you believe they can help you accomplish this by verbalizing cues, assigning fancy drills from their arsenal, using the latest technology, following a systematic approach, and taking 100 swings a day.

After years of trial and error: I still haven't identified that magic trick.

However, I have figured out that the body is responsible for every element required to produce a rotational movement pattern. Drills and cues alone can improve the explosiveness and power you currently possess, yet they will not produce gains.

Drills "can" optimize, they don't create. When technology documents your increased ball exit speed after working on mechanics, you didn't get stronger, you became a more efficient mover.

The Truth

In order for you to be the best version of yourself, there must be a combination of the body and the mind. The mind equals the hitting component (decision-making). The body equals the swing component (mechanics). The swing can be broken down into four main areas. Here's where it gets complicated, and why most systematic approaches fail...

THE 1728 COMBINATIONS PROBLEM

THE STANCE

Think about your starting position. Most players develop their stance in one of three ways: observation (watching others and mimicking what looks cool), comfort (developing their own stance based on what feels natural, your preference), or coaching (establishing a stance based on how they're coached, my least favorite).

In my opinion, you should be properly assessed before anyone messes with your comfort zone. You may not consider your starting position important, the problem is, your start can tremendously impact your finish.

Let me show you the mathematical nightmare of systematic coaching:

1,728 possible combinations at a minimum. I am sure you could include other components or options.

In addition, we haven't even considered how you move out of or through these positions.

Table 6.1 - Mechanical Combinations

Component	Options	Count
Hand Position	High, Low, Forward, Back, Proximal, Distal	6
Feet Positions	Wide, Narrow, Open, Closed	4
Weight Distribution	Back, Center, Forward	3
Stance Combinations	$6 \times 4 \times 3$	72
Load/Stride Types	Leg Lift, Toe Tap, No Stride, Open to Close	4
Weight Shifts	Shift, No Shift	2
Foot Down Methods	Toe-Heel, Heel-Toe, Simultaneous	3
TOTAL COMBINATIONS	$72 \times 4 \times 2 \times 3$	1,728

RHYTHM - THE BRIDGE BETWEEN MECHANIC AND TIMING

"A pitcher's job is to disrupt rhythm and timing."

- Unknown

"A hitter's job is to stay in rhythm and be on time."

- Rogerick A. Thompson

I find it intriguing, when the primary job of the hitter is to stay in rhythm, this element of hitting is never discussed with hitters!

Rhythm is the link between mechanics and timing. It is also the key to recognition and adjustability. It's like the plus symbol in a simple addition problem, completing the mechanical task.

Table 6.2 - The Bridge

Concept	Visual Representation	Description
The Equation	Mechanics $\longrightarrow$ (Rhythm) $\longrightarrow$ Timing = Path $\longrightarrow$ Max Exit Velocity	Rhythm acts as the bridge, it's not a step, it's the connector.
Meaning		When rhythm flows, timing syncs naturally, enhances recognition, creating an efficient path and higher exit velocities.

FALL BALL IN STARKVILLE

With the regular season over and missing softball, I seized a great opportunity to travel north for some 2024 fall ball. Mississippi State University was the destination.

After watching the players swing a few times, I was pretty intrigued by one UCLA transfer. "Who is that?" I asked Coach Ricketts. "That's Lexi Sosa," Ricketts said. "I really like that swing," I responded. Ricketts indicated her swing gets out of control sometimes. "She may have better control if she was smoother with her rhythm," I offered.

I filed that observation away. Rhythm issues. A common problem. Fixable if the player understands the source.

SEC SPRING SERIES: TEXAS

Fast-forward to spring. The Texas series. I'm sitting behind the backstop, my favorite spot. This is the place to be if you want to see the game clearly. You can watch the vertical and horizontal breaks of the pitches. It gives you a different view than from the side. My favorite view is the pitch location and bat path.

I do the same thing every game. I watched all 18 batters. Three reasons: How can I attack them? How can I assist them? What can I learn?

On a curveball thrown to Lexi, I thought she was a little quick. I really locked in on the next at-bat. I say to myself, her rhythm is off.

THE CONVERSATION I DIDN'T EXPECT

As I was waiting for the next doubleheader game, Lexi walked up to me. "Did I get around that ball?" she asked.

I immediately thought. *What? I don't know you like that. How do I give my opinion without knowing how you'll process what I say?*

The Problem

Here's the challenge with giving on-the-spot feedback: you don't know the player's connection or learning language. You also don't know their trust level or whether they want affirmation or correction.

One wrong word can create confusion right before their next at-bat. Yet, I wanted to answer the question she asked.

The Response

I calmly said, "It looks like your rhythm is off. You may be starting too late."

"So I need to start earlier?" Lexi asked.

"You're a high-level player. You know when to start," was my final statement.

I wasn't going to tell her HOW to time. I was going to make her aware of WHAT was happening. She had to figure out her solution.

Possibly, telling her exactly when to start could mess up her natural timing even more. She needed awareness, not instruction.

A Few Minutes Later

Same pitch location. This time? Nice and smooth. See ya. It's out of here.

The Truth

That home run wasn't because I fixed her mechanics. I didn't touch her swing. I didn't change her stance. I didn't adjust her bat path. I simply gave her awareness about her rhythm. She made the adjustment herself.

Elite players like Lexi don't need you to solve their problems, they need you to identify the source. That's the difference between fixing a player (telling them exactly what to do) and empowering a player (helping them discover their own solution).

Lexi already had the physical tools. She already had the swing. She already had the talent. What she needed was awareness that her rhythm was off. Once she had that awareness, her body knew what to do.

This is why rhythm and timing work is so critical. It's not always about mechanics. Sometimes it's just about rhythm, about when you start, about being in sync with the pitch.

THE LESSON

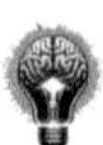When you see a player with a great swing producing inconsistent results, ask yourself: Is it their swing? Or is it their rhythm? Is it their mechanics? Or is it their timing? Is it their body position? Or is it their mind?

Most of the time, it's rhythm and timing. Not positions and paths. Rhythm and timing can be adjusted in seconds if the player has awareness. Mechanics? Those take weeks.

The Challenge

Next time you struggle in a game, before you rush to change your mechanics, ask yourself: Was my rhythm off? Did I start too early or too late? Was my rhythm too fast or too slow? Was I in sync with the pitcher or off sync with the ball?

Sometimes the fastest fix isn't a mechanical change. It's a rhythm adjustment.

Lexi proved it in one at-bat.

Let's take a look at the load, weight shift and foot down options. Elements that can impact your rhythm and, or timing.

The Load And Stride (4 Options)

Leg lift: A more athletic move that serves as a rhythm, timing, and adjustability tool. The leg lift may be required for smaller players to increase power production. Larger players can eliminate this move and still exceed power produced by some smaller ones'. This move is often removed from players for one of the following reasons: too much head movement, late timing, or contradicts the belief of the instructor or coach.

Toe tap: Provides rhythm, timing, and adjustability with a reduction in body movement. Often suggested when coaches want to eliminate the leg lift.

No stride: Can be performed with heel up or heel down. Popular for players who feel they need to see the ball better as they face better pitching. I've seen it forced on players due to late timing. This is also popular as a two-strike approach.

The challenge: having two different timing triggers if this is only used in two-strike situations.

Open to close: Some players are instructed to stand square to the plate. The square stance doesn't work for everyone. Closing the stance provides some players better barrel direction and prevents over-rotation.

The challenge: creating a lean over the plate producing a positive attack and making your barrel vulnerable to the up and in pitch.

Think about the variety of load and stride combinations!

Weight Shift (2 Options)

Shift: A majority of players have some level of shift. Some shifts are greater than others. However, there are exceptions (like Aaron Judge's move). The shift is essential for some players as it relates to putting force into the ground and torso positioning to align the barrel with the pitch.

No Shift: Popular amongst those who feel staying back and eliminating any type of head movement.

Foot Down (2 Options)

Prior to rotation, you must get to a stable leg. There are two ways this occurs: toe-heel-down method, or heel-toe-down simultaneously method.

The Problem

If you fall into a system approach, it may be a challenge for you to experience the best version of yourself.

Think about it: your coach has a system. It works for some players. Maybe even most players. So they apply it to everyone.

You're not everyone. You might be combination #142. The system is built for combination #37.

So what happens? You spend months forcing your body into positions that feel unnatural. Your timing gets disrupted. Your rhythm disappears. Your confidence erodes. Then everyone wonders why you're struggling when "the system works for everyone else."

The Truth

Here's the uncomfortable reality that most coaches won't admit. There is no one-size-fits-all mechanical solution. Think of it like shoes. Nike makes great shoes. They work for millions of people. If you force someone with size 12 feet into size 9 shoes and tell them to "just make it work," what happens?

They can't run properly. They can't jump. They develop injuries. They underperform. The shoe doesn't fit. Your mechanics are the same. The system might be excellent, though if it doesn't fit YOUR body, YOUR timing, YOUR natural movement patterns, it becomes a prison instead of a platform.

CHALLENGE #1: THE COMBINATION DISCOVERY

This week, return to the mechanical combination table, identify your component option.

Did you choose these positions or were they assigned to you? Do they feel natural or forced? Have you ever tested alternative combinations? Has a coach ever told you your natural movement is "wrong"?

Am I being coached as an individual or processed through a system? Even if you have the right mechanical combination, there's still something missing...

WHAT TIME MATTERS

Timing

You understand time, but can you tell time, to be on time for the pitch you know is coming?

Think about it: how often have you seen players be late or early from at-bat to at-bat for specific speed ranges? Probably pretty often.

Why is this? If both in life and hitting, as we mature, we discuss the importance of time, why don't so many hitters develop the timing component?

The Sis Bates Revelation

Fall 2022. I had the opportunity to sit down with my favorite shortstop, Sis Bates. I'm always curious about how the elite accomplish things.

So I asked: "Would you sit on a changeup with less than two strikes?" "Yes," Sis replied. "How did you determine your later timing to have success against that pitch?" Her response: "I could just feel it!"

Well, this was a new one.

The Most Important Questions You Can Ask Yourself

Just like anything else, timing is an individualized element of hitting. Let me challenge you with three questions. Answer them honestly.

Question 1: When do you start? Most players say: "When the pitcher gets to a specific location."

Question 2: What do you call the start? Typical response: "When I load."

Question 3: When do you go forward? Can you answer immediately? Or are you not sure?

The Problem

Some hitters time the pitcher when they should be timing the ball.

Here's what I don't do: tell players "how to time". Here's what I will do: help you understand how you time.

There are players who are successful starting off the pitcher, with the forward move determined by the ball. Application of this method is very dangerous for players with the continuous load-and-shift pattern. You know the type: loads up, and at the top of the load, goes right into a shift.

This method can result in early ball timing, creating a lunge on the outside off-speed or changeup.

The Truth

What is not often discovered among hitters is how they time. Think of timing like music. Some musicians count beats: "1-2-3-4." Others feel the rhythm naturally. Neither is wrong, yet you need to know which one you are.

If you're a "counter" trying to play like a "feeler," you'll always be off tempo. If you're a "feeler" being forced to count, you'll lose your natural rhythm.

Realizing how you time yourself is the foundation of hunting speed and location. If you can apply this to your game, you can reduce two of the primary miss types: early and late.

How do you time? Timing is essential for those who cannot master the bat-to-ball path. What if your path is already dialed in?

Table 6.3 - Timing Elements Checklist

Timing Element	When It Happens	How to Identify	Why It Matters
Load Start	Before pitcher's release	First backward movement	Establishes rhythm
Forward Shift	After load	Weight begins moving forward	Aligns body for power
Foot Down Decision	Just before commitment	Front foot lands	Key timing checkpoint
Rotation Trigger	Point of no return	Hips begin to open	Releases power sequence

THE IMPORTANCE OF PATH

On this Sunday, I received a message from Hannah Jo inquiring about a hitting lesson. I asked her to send me videos she had challenges with, and some she was proud of. After looking at the four videos, it was obvious she had a problem up and in. This is something I believe should be addressed immediately prior to entering the SEC as a 2026 freshman at Mississippi State University.

She possessed the power; we just needed to become more precise with the barrel in a specific area.

A few weeks later, I had my first experience working with this future Mississippi State Bulldog. She walked through the door, and I asked, "So, tell me about the rise ball." "I don't swing at it," Hannah Jo said.

Remember my Georgia and LSU camp discovery, where the best players did not swing at vulnerable strike zone areas?

"Well, if you don't learn how to hit the rise ball, coaches will go right after you. That area will be discovered", I said.

We went to work. Right to the area she avoids in the game. A combination of dialogue and tweaking to determine what worked based on her movement style. After the three-hour session ended, I told her, "You will be playing in the SEC in less than two years. Why wait to test what you just proved you can do. Your next game, hunt the rise and if it doesn't work we will assess the challenges."

A few days later, during the second at-bat, I received four videos from her father: Pitch 1 - Riseball - foul straight back. Pitch 2 - Curveball - take for a strike. Pitch 3 - Riseball - take for a ball. Pitch 4 - Riseball - see ya!

Just a few days ago elevated pitches were a problem. On this day, she can now punish them. It is such a joy when players understand the value of bat path. This is one of the main ingredients of hunting pitches.

The Alignment Principle

If you don't value path, it's possible your career may be on the wrong path. I prefer to also call this alignment, getting the round bat in the line of the round ball with the highest level of efficiency. When this occurs, you'll see your contact percentage increase.

Here's the significance: the perfection of timing is not required.

The Grade System

A+ Path, Imperfect Timing: A swing that produces an A+ path that's a little late will produce a contact point on the handle side of the sweet spot. An A+ path that's a little early will have a contact point on the end cap part of the bat.

C+ Path, Perfect Timing Required: A swing that produces a C+ path with a positive or negative attack angle may require A-timing. When the path of the bat and ball are not aligned, timing must be closer to perfection.

The Problem

Most players chase perfect timing instead of perfect path. You work on "being on time" in the cage. You feel great when you square balls up down the middle at a known speed.

Then you get to the game. The speeds vary. The locations move. The sequences change. The break is horizontal. The break is vertical. Your "perfect timing" evaporates. If your path is elite, you have a margin for error.

The Truth

Consider the task you're attempting to accomplish, bat-to-ball alignment. Think about your misses (over and under). When the goal is to put the equator of the bat on the equator of the ball: A slight miss above → hard ground ball. A slight miss on the bottom → line drive over the infield's head.

Attempting to match the center of the bat with the center of the ball will still result in productive outcomes, even when you miss.

How can you produce consistent results when you will consistently produce imperfect time and path?

The answer: "Pursue perfection."

Think of it like archery. Professional archers don't hit the bullseye every time. Their consistent form means even their "misses" stay on target. Your path is your form. Perfect it, and your misses become productive outs or hits instead of weak grounders and pop-ups.

CHALLENGE #2: THE PATH AUDIT

For your next three cage sessions, focus ONLY on path (ignore timing).

Session 1: Down the Middle. Take 20 swings at a consistent speed down the middle, video from the side, grade your path: A, C, F. Note: Where does your barrel enter the zone? Where does it exit?

Session 2: Location Variability. Take 20 swings at varied locations (same speed), video from the side, grade your path on each location. Note: Does your path change match the pitch height?

Session 3: The Analysis. Compare videos. Ask yourself: Is my path consistent across locations? Does my barrel travel in a straight line through the ball? Do I have the same path on good timing and bad timing? Would my misses still produce quality contact?

Be honest. Since in competition, you won't have the luxury of perfect timing. You need a path that produces results even when you're slightly off.

Here's where most players make their biggest mistake...

CORRECTION AND/OR COMPENSATION

THE POWER 5 COMMIT BATTING SEVENTH

GiGi wasn't your typical travel ball player. She enjoyed playing the game, yet she also enjoyed life. Her God-given talent, speed, strength, athleticism, gave her the opportunity to not have to put in as much work as others.

However, we know how that story goes when it comes to hitting. Talent can carry you, until it can't.

The Commitment

Prior to her senior year in high school, GiGi committed to Power 5, Big 12, Baylor University. A program with a yearly presence in the top 25 rankings.

Her high school team? The reigning state champions in Mississippi.

Everything was set up perfectly. Senior year. Committed player. Championship team.

The Problem

The season started rocky. GiGi was batting anywhere from seventh through eighth.

Let that sink in for a moment. A Power 5 commit batting seventh on her high school team, in her senior year. Your teammates know you're committed to Baylor, college coaches are watching, your family is in the stands, and you're contributing nothing. What would that do to your mentality if you were in the same situation?

I can only imagine the questions running through her head: "Did Baylor make a mistake?" "Am I even good enough?" "What happened to me?"

The Phone Call

Like a lot of cases, after not hearing from GiGi for a while, my phone rang.

We set up the next session to go to work. She walked in the cage, I didn't start with mechanics. I didn't start with drills. I didn't start with a motivational speech.

I asked her one question: "Are you willing to do what it takes to be the best version of yourself?"

I knew what was coming. I knew GiGi was going to have to do some uncomfortable things. She didn't have much time. This was midseason. The championship window was closing.

The Decision

Here's what makes GiGi's story different from everything I teach in this book: This was not my typical approach. In Chapter 6, I tell you to make corrections in the off-season and compensations in-season. GiGi did both. We did all these things in a compressed timeline, while games were happening and as the pressure was mounting.

Why did we make this exception? She was broken, and she had nothing to lose. Sometimes, when you're broken down mentally, that's the only time you're willing to rebuild.

The Process

I won't lie to you. It was brutal, not physically, but strategically.

We addressed mechanical corrections she'd been avoiding for years, timing compensations she needed immediately, rhythm issues that were destroying her confidence, and approach problems that left her guessing.

All in a compressed timeline. All while games were happening. All while the pressure was mounting.

This wasn't ideal. It was necessary.

GiGi was already struggling. Her confidence was already shot. Her production was already terrible.

What did she have to lose?

The Breakthrough

By the end of the season, GiGi had moved to the front of the lineup. She helped lead her high school team back to another state championship.

The Truth About Gigi's Story

The significance of GiGi's turnaround, she had to be broken down mentally before she could be built back up.

This is uncomfortable to talk about. We don't like admitting that sometimes struggle is necessary. Sometimes rock bottom is where transformation begins.

GiGi had relied on talent her entire career. She'd never had to face adversity. She'd never had to question herself. Until senior year, when suddenly her talent wasn't enough. That breakdown, painful as it was, created the opening for real change.

The Exception, Not The Rule

GiGi's story is an exception.

I don't recommend in-season corrections and compensations simultaneously for most players. It's risky. It's uncomfortable. It requires desperation. Sometimes, when you're already at rock bottom, the risk is worth it. Where else can you go but up? A case where the desire to change was greater than the desire to remain the same!

The Lesson

GiGi's story teaches us something most coaches don't want to admit. Sometimes comfort is the enemy of growth. As long as GiGi was comfortable, even if that meant batting seventh, she wasn't going to change. She was going to keep doing what she'd always done.

Things changed when the discomfort of staying the same became greater than the discomfort of changing. That's when transformation happened.

The Question

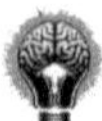 Am I comfortable being uncomfortable enough to change? Not just mechanically. Mentally.

Are you willing to be broken down before you're built back up? Are you willing to question everything you've relied on? Are you willing to do uncomfortable things in a compressed timeline if that's what it takes?

GiGi answered yes. She went from batting seventh to leading her team to a championship.

The question is: How would you address your need to change?

THE OFF-SEASON WINDOW

MOVEMENT AND POSITION CORRECTIVES AND COMPENSATIONS

The off-season is one of those opportunities where you can make the greatest progression gains. These gains typically start with an assessment from the previous season and returning better than you left.

Here's the question almost nobody asks: Do I need a correction or a compensation? Most players don't even know there's a difference.

The Lana J Experience

During the 2025 Women's College World Series, Lana J batted in the four hole against the University of Texas. It wasn't surprising how they were going to pitch her based on her at-bats in Clearwater versus Jordy Bahl and against Texas shortly thereafter.

I had the opportunity to share with Lana prior to the regular season Texas series: "Mike White is a great pitching coach, and Steve Singleton is a great hitting coach. They are going to attack you in the same areas Jordy Bahl had success with you."

Fast-forward to the WCWS, Lana knew what was going to occur. The same thing that happened in the regular season. Mike White stuck with the plan of going down and in on Lana. After a few at-bats, she made an adjustment that resulted in the hardest ball hit in the 2025 WCWS.

To this day, she would tell you there were problems getting it into the air, and when she did hit the ball, it was hit directly at someone.

The Correction

When Lana entered the cage that summer, the goal was to first address the correction, which is movement or position related. She had slowly transitioned to an open stance over the years combined with a toe tap. When she commenced her load and closed her stance, the torso drifted over the plate. This repositioning impacted how the barrel would come through the zone and lose direction.

Therefore, we proceeded with addressing the retention of posture to improve barrel direction. However, we did not vacate what she does well.

Like most players who desire to become the best version of themselves, Lana wasn't putting in the work to feel good, she was present to get better.

The Problem

Most players don't understand the difference between corrections and compensations. Corrections address the root cause (movement or position related). Compensations adjust to work around a limitation you can't, won't or don't have time to fix.

Think of it like a car. Correction: Fixing a flat tire by removing the nail and patching it up. Compensations: Leaving the nail in and adding Fix-A-Flat.

One solves the problem. The other masks it.

Most players spend their entire careers compensating since they never identified what actually needed to be corrected.

The Truth

In a conversation with Josh Johnson (at the time Mississippi State Softball pitching coach) about Sis Bates and her performance, he indicated: "Athletes make their greatest gains in the off-season."

That resonated with me and gave me two different perspectives.

Perspective 1 (Collegiate Players): During your summer break, you should have a clear understanding of what needs to improve, what is the source of the improvement barrier, and what is the proper solution.

Perspective 2 (High School Players): What are your weaknesses that are micro now, but will become macro later? Will you close the gap between where you are and where you need to be before arriving on campus?

Identifying the source and applying solutions are paramount to becoming a better version of yourself. Even though the sources are mechanical related in a majority of cases, they can also be timing or approach related as well.

The number one step in the process of corrective identification is the identification of the problem.

"Address the root, not the fruit." You can't fix what you haven't properly diagnosed. Here's what most players miss...

THE CLOSING WINDOW

The 80/20 Rule

There is a time to discuss and simulate the game, and there is a time to play the game.

As Tony Baldwin, University of Georgia's coach, shared with me once: "We apply the 80/20 rule." Fall Focus: 80% skill acquisition, 20% playing the game. Spring Focus (after Christmas break): 20% skill acquisition, 80% game play.

The Problem

Most players don't understand that the window for corrections closes.

You likely can't make major mechanical changes in the middle of the season. The risk is too high. The time is too limited. The pressure is too great.

Think of it like construction. You can renovate a house during the off-season. Once people are living in it, you're limited to small repairs and adjustments. You can't tear down walls when the family needs a place to sleep.

Prior to the window closing, it is essential to correctly apply correctives to each individual player. There must be important decisions made prior to returning to campus or starting the season for high school players.

Do I correct or compensate? Can you correct?

Let me show you what this looks like at the highest level…

THE BAT FLIP QUEEN EXCEPTION

THE PLAYER WHO CHANGED THE GAME

It was 2019 when the two-way player, Sam Show of Oklahoma State University, brought additional excitement to the game of softball with the bat flip heard around the world. A reason I love softball. Benches would have cleared in baseball.

I had the pleasure of talking with Sam about sitting on speed and location at the 2021 NFCA convention. How exciting it was to discuss hitting and pitching with a two-way player. Felt like my typical exciting conversation with a great player or coach, but two skills in one conversation.

Four years later, I realized that was just a typical conversation. Until it wasn't.

The Message I Didn't Expect

During her professional season in Japan, I got a notification from Sam Show. I thought someone was playing a joke.

"I was hoping we could have a call and talk hitting," the message read. "Sam! Don't play with me! Are you serious?" I responded.

She was serious.

The Problem

We discussed her approach, game planning strategies, what she was feeling in her swing, and what her coaching staff wanted.

How her positioning and timing had changed. How what worked in college wasn't translating to professional competition in Japan. Together, we reviewed the difference between her 2019 swing and her 2025 swing.

The intent: identify what she was willing to do to create more consistency and better adjustability with two strikes.

Sam Show, one of the most talented players in college softball history, was struggling with consistency at the professional level. Not due to her lack of talent. Not because she didn't work hard.

Since what got her to the pros wasn't enough to dominate at the pros. She had to level up.

The Decision

Here's where Sam made the choice that separates good players from great ones.

She could have found quick compensations to survive the season (Option A) or commit to corrections that would require uncomfortable change (Option B).

Most players choose Option A. It's safer. It's faster. It keeps you comfortable. Sam chose Option B.

The Commitment

Sam went to work. Even though some positions and feels were unfamiliar, she stayed with it. This is one thing nobody talks about:

> Corrections feel wrong before they feel right. Your body fights you. Your mind questions you. Every at-bat feels like you're learning to hit all over again.

Sam trusted the process. Weeks went by. Not days. Weeks.

The Truth

I was able to see barrel path improvements and position improvements as the season progressed. Her improvement strategy started with a commitment to correction, not compensation.

As a result? A higher level of consistency. Here's what made Sam's story different from most players:

The Exception That Proves The Rule

Remember everything we've discussed in this chapter about timing windows? Off-season equals correction window. In-season equals compensation window.

Sam broke that rule. It worked.

Why? Since she had three things most players don't: elite body awareness (as a two-way player, Sam understood movement patterns better than most. She could feel the difference between correct and incorrect positions faster than the average player), professional environment (she had access to daily training, video review, and coaching support that allowed her to work through corrections during the season), and unwavering commitment (she trusted the process even when results didn't come immediately.

Even when it felt uncomfortable. Even when compensation would have been easier, Sam made a commitment to make the necessary improvements.

The Lesson

Most players reading this will think: "Sam did corrections in-season, so I can too!"

Wrong. Sam Show is an exception, not the rule.

For every Sam Show who successfully makes corrections in-season, there are a hundred players who try to correct mid-season, struggle through the discomfort, lose confidence, lose playing time, and never recover.

The lesson isn't: "Make corrections in-season like Sam."

The lesson is: "If you're going to make corrections in-season, you better be as committed, self-aware, and supported as Sam was."

The Reality Check

Do I have elite body awareness? Do I have daily access to coaching and video support? Can I afford weeks of discomfort without losing my position? Am I willing to sacrifice short-term results for long-term improvement?

If you answered "no" to any of these, stick to the rule: Corrections in the off-season. Compensations in-season.

The Professional Standard

Here's what Sam's story reveals about the difference between college and professional softball.

In college, Sam's natural talent and elite swing carried her. She could get away with mechanical inefficiencies since she was that good.

In Japan? Against professional pitchers who could locate with precision and pitching coaches who studied her tendencies? Her weaknesses got exposed. She had a choice to adapt or plateau. She chose to adapt. She did it the hard way, through correction, not compensation.

Challenge: The Sam Show Standard

Before you attempt in-season corrections, complete this assessment.

Part 1: Self-Awareness Check. Can you feel the difference between correct and incorrect positions without video? Do you understand the source of your mechanical issue? Can you articulate what needs to change and why?

Part 2: Support System Check. Do you have daily access to quality coaching? Can you review video after every at-bat? Do you have someone holding you accountable to the correction?

Part 3: Commitment Check. Are you willing to struggle for weeks, not days? Can you maintain confidence through poor results? Will you stick with the correction even when compensation seems easier?

Part 4: Risk Assessment. Can you afford to lose playing time during the adjustment? Is your position secure enough to weather the storm? Do you have the luxury of development time?

If you can't answer "yes" to all these questions, follow the standard rule: Wait for the off-season window.

The Truth About Exceptions

Sam Show's story is inspiring. It's proof that corrections can work in-season if you're committed enough. It's an exception, not a template.

For every one Sam Show, there are countless players who tried the same thing and lost confidence, lost playing time, lost their position, and regressed instead of improved.

The difference? Sam had the awareness, support, and commitment required to make it work. Most players don't, and that's okay. That's why the off-season window exists.

The Final Word

If you're a professional player or an elite college athlete with Sam Show-level self-awareness and support, go ahead, make corrections when you need them.

If you're a high school player, a college freshman, or anyone without that level of support and security? Stick to the plan. Corrections in the off-season. Compensations in-season. Production over perfection when games matter.

Sam Show proved corrections can work in-season. She also proved that it requires exceptional circumstances and commitment. Don't mistake her exception for your rule.

The Sosa Adjustment Revisited

Remember Lexi Sosa from earlier in this chapter? The rhythm adjustment that led to an immediate home run? That wasn't the only adjustment Lexi made during the season.

Also in conference play, I watched as an opposing pitcher discovered her vulnerability: down and in. Her natural bat path couldn't handle that location. It cut across instead of getting through.

In game one of the series, she didn't reach base. Talking to Coach Ricketts after the game, I mentioned: "If she just swings at her toes, her bat may run into it tomorrow." From behind the back stop, you could get a great view of that path.

Game two, first at-bat: robbed over the fence. Next at-bat: crushed. The same pitch she couldn't touch the day before became her power zone the day after. Compensation, not correction. Strategic adjustment, not mechanical overhaul.

It kept her productive when it mattered most.

THE SEATTLE TRIP

THE SERIES YOU CIRCLE ON THE CALENDAR

One of those weekends you look forward to all season: watching Lana J and Stanford.

This wasn't just any series. A conference matchup with the best pitcher in the nation: NiJaree Canady.

I circled this one on the calendar the moment the schedule was released. Getting to see Lana J face NiJa. The young lady we discussed in the cage during the holidays. I wouldn't miss it.

Day Three: The Hangout

On day three of the series, Chad and I hung out with the fabulous four: Ruby, Syd, Brooklyn, and Lana.

As we were discussing the game, Brooklyn said something that caught my attention: "That NiJa!"

The tone said everything. Frustration. Respect. Maybe a little fear. I'm thinking: "What's going on here?"

The Problem

Here's the reality: NiJa is not just good. She's generational. The kind of pitcher who makes elite hitters look average.

Brooklyn had faced her. She knew what she was up against. She was in her own head about the match up.

The Response

"You got this," I said.

Then I reminded her of something from earlier in the season. A swing and miss where she had the flattest bat path ever. What a hack it was. Honestly, one of the best swings and misses I'd ever seen.

Why bring up a swing and miss? Since it showed me what her body could do when she committed to a path. "All you have to do is swing..." I mentioned the adjustment.

Not a long explanation. Not a mechanical breakdown. Just a simple cue that paired up with her movement type. On to the stadium Chad and I went.

A Few Hours Later

Brooklyn steps in the box.

There it was: one of the few base hits against the best pitcher in the nation.

It Wasn't Magic

Here's what people don't understand: the cue was quite simple.

I knew every swing on that team. I'd watched them all season. I understood their movement patterns, their timing, their tendencies.

Brooklyn made a statement that revealed she was a little nervous. I just gave a response that paired up with her movement type. That's it. No complex overhaul. No mechanical deep dive. Just awareness paired with a simple cue.

The Truth Behind The Hit

After the game, I asked: "What was your approach?"

"There were two things," Brooklyn said. "I didn't want NiJa stomping me, and I thought about what you said."

Let that sink in.

Two things: competitive fire (I don't want to get dominated) and strategic adjustment (the cue I gave her).

Not mechanics. Not swing positions. Not bat path analysis.

Mind + Simple Adjustment = Production.

The Elite Player Reality

Here's the truth: a lot of young ladies at that level don't need much. They have the physical tools. They have the swing. They have the talent.

What they need is awareness of what's happening, a simple cue that matches their movement, and permission to trust what they already know.

Brooklyn didn't need me to rebuild her swing. She needed me to remind her of what her body could already do.

The Outcome Vs. Method Principle

When the game is on the line, production is what matters, not process.

Think of it like a surgeon. They have a preferred technique for every procedure. When complications arise mid-surgery, they don't stick to the plan, they adapt to save the patient. The outcome matters more than the method.

Brooklyn could have stuck to her "proper" swing and gone 0-for-3 against NiJa, or she could make a strategic adjustment, get a hit, and contribute to her team's success. She chose production. It worked.

The Compensation In Action

What I gave Brooklyn wasn't a correction. It was compensation.

A strategic adjustment to handle a specific challenge (the best pitcher in the nation) without overhauling her entire approach.

This is exactly what we've been discussing. Corrections take time. It happens in the off-season. Address root causes. Compensations are immediate. happen in-season. Solve specific problems.

Brooklyn needed compensation. Her swing was not broken, she needed a tool to handle an elite pitcher in a high-pressure moment.

The Lesson For Players

When you're facing the best pitcher, you've ever seen, you have two choices.

Option A: Stick to your natural swing and hope it works.

Option B: Make a strategic adjustment based on what your body can do.

Brooklyn chose Option B. She got a hit off the best pitcher in the nation.

That's not luck. That's strategic thinking combined with physical execution.

Lesson For Instructors Before College

Here's what Brooklyn's story teaches about coaching elite players.

Know your players' movements: I knew Brooklyn's swing. I knew what her body could do. I'd seen the swing-and-miss earlier in the season that showed me her capability.

I can't give effective cues if you don't know your players' movement patterns.

Keep it simple. I didn't give Brooklyn a 10-minute explanation. I gave her one cue that connected to something she'd already done. Elite players don't need complexity. They need clarity.

Match the cue to the mover. The adjustment I suggested worked since it matched Brooklyn's movement type. The same cue might not work for Syd or Lana.

Individualization matters.

Trust the competitor. Brooklyn had two motivations: not wanting to get dominated and executing the adjustment. I didn't need to manufacture motivation. I just needed to give her a tool. Elite players are already motivated. Our job is to equip them.

The Pressure Performance Principle

Good players stick to what's comfortable, even when it's not working.

Great players adapt strategically when the moment demands it.

Brooklyn was willing to make an adjustment against the best pitcher in the nation, In a conference series with the game on the line. That's not just talent. That's mental toughness combined with strategic thinking.

The Question You Need To Answer

When you face the best pitcher, you've ever seen, will you stick to your comfort zone and hope for the best, or make a strategic adjustment and give yourself a chance?

Brooklyn made her choice. She got a hit.

What will you choose?

Challenge: The Elite Adjustment

For your next high-pressure at-bat (playoffs, championship, elite opponent).

Before the game: Identify one strategic adjustment you can make if your natural swing isn't working. Practice the adjustment in the cage so your body knows the feel. Trust that you can execute it when needed.

During the game: Assess after your first at-bat: Is my natural approach working? If not, implement the strategic adjustment. Commit fully, no halfway compensations.

After the game: Did the adjustment work? What did you learn about your ability to adapt under pressure? What will you do differently next time?

Elite players have answers. Average players have excuses. Which one are you?

The Final Truth

Brooklyn's hit off NiJa wasn't magic.

It was awareness of what her body could do, a simple cue matched to her movement, competitive fire to not get dominated, and willingness to adjust strategically.

Most importantly, it was production when it mattered most. It wasn't the prettiest swing or the most mechanically perfect approach. Just a base hit against the best pitcher in the nation. At the end of the day, that's all that shows up in the box score.

THE AARON JUDGE DILEMMA

THE 95 MPH MOMENT

During the 2025 division series (while writing this book), Aaron Judge hit his only home run in the postseason, a 95 mph pitch up and in, not for a strike.

This was not an area he performed well in.

As I compared his movement patterns from 2024 to 2025, there were not any noticeable changes. However, there were some distinct differences in the numbers.

The Compensation Hypothesis

So, what was the difference?

From afar, it appears he made a compensation by pulling his hands in sooner to get the barrel on the ball.

You can see the difference in the overall batting average performance. Not only that, but it also appears the attack angle got flatter, and the ball exit speed average was lowered. Did Judge reduce the aggressiveness up and in to increase barrel accuracy?

Maybe I'll have the opportunity to ask one day.

The Problem

Was there ever a correction considered?

If so, was it too extreme for his body type, too late in his career to implement, or too risky given his already impressive production?

After all, he did put up impressive numbers in both 2024 and 2025.

The Truth

Aaron Judge likely had a performance improvement plan in place for the off-season to address vulnerable areas within the strike zone.

You would think the same approach would be taken with high school and college players. Identify vulnerabilities, look for corrective opportunities, (if none are discovered) identify compensations at the close of the corrective window, and develop ability to apply compensations prior to competition window opening.

Think about this: if a player hitting 50+ home runs per season has to choose between correction (which might disrupt everything) and compensation (which maintains production while minimizing damage), what should he choose?

This is the correction vs. compensation decision every player "should" face.

THE DECISION YOU MUST MAKE

CORRECTION OR COMPENSATION?

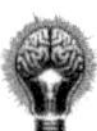 You're standing at a crossroads right now. The off-season is approaching (or already here). You have vulnerabilities that were exposed last season.

You have two options.

Option 1: The Correction Path. Identify the root cause of your vulnerability, address movement or position patterns, potentially disrupt your timing and rhythm temporarily, risk short-term struggle for long-term gain, commit to the 80/20 Summer-fall focus, and trust the process even when it feels uncomfortable.

Option 2: The Compensation Path. Accept the mechanical limitation, develop workarounds to minimize exposure, maintain current production levels, adjust approach to avoid vulnerable areas, focus on optimizing what already works, and live with the hole but reduce its impact.

The Problem

Most players try to do both at once.

They want the correction benefits without the correction commitment. They want to maintain their current production while completely rebuilding their swing. It doesn't work that way.

Think of it like learning a new language. You can't speak fluently in your new language while still speaking your native language. There's a transition period where you're uncomfortable, slow, and making mistakes. That transition period is where most players quit.

They start making corrections in the fall. It feels uncomfortable. Timing is off. Contact quality drops. Confidence wavers.

So, they bail. They go back to their old pattern. They convince themselves that I'll just compensate and work around it. They never develop the compensation strategy either. They just drift.

The Truth

Here's what separates elite players from good players: Elite players commit fully to one path or the other.

If they're going to correct, they correct with full commitment during the 80/20 fall window. They accept the temporary discomfort knowing the window will close. If they're going to compensate, they develop a strategic compensation plan. They don't just "avoid" their holes, they address them.

Good players do neither. They dabble in corrections without committing. They hope their holes won't get exposed. They pray the pitcher makes a mistake. Hope is not a strategy.

CHALLENGE #3: THE OFF-SEASON DECISION

This is the most important challenge in this chapter. It will determine your trajectory for the next season.

Step 1: Identify Your Vulnerability. Answer these questions: What zone or pitch type got you out most last season? Was it mechanical, timing, or approach related? Did it get worse as the season progressed? Do you have time to fix the root cause?

Step 2: Correction or Compensation? If you choose correction: What is the specific movement or position that needs to change? How long will the correction take to feel natural? Do you have access to quality coaching during the transition? When does your correction window close?

If you choose compensation: What specific adjustment will you make to minimize vulnerability exposure? How will you adjust your approach to hunt your strengths? How will you practice the compensation strategy?

Step 3: Commit. Write down your choice. Share it with your coach, your parents, your trainer. Then commit 100%. No dabbling. No hedging. No bailout plans. One path. Full commitment.

At the end of the off-season, you'll either have addressed the root cause and eliminated the vulnerability or have developed a strategic compensation that minimizes its impact. You won't be drifting anymore.

The Lana J Epilogue

Remember Lana's story from the WCWS? She came into the summer with a clear correction need: torso position impacting barrel direction. She could have compensated. She could have just adjusted her approach to avoid down-and-in pitches. She could have lived with the hole.

She chose correction.

She spent the fall addressing the root cause. It felt uncomfortable. Her timing was off initially. Contact quality varied. There were moments of doubt. Fortunately, she committed to the 80/20 fall window. She trusted the process. She stayed with the correction.

When the window closed and spring arrived, the correction had become her new normal.

The down-and-in pitch that plagued her at the WCWS was no longer a hole. She didn't avoid it, she fixed it. That's the power of choosing correction over compensation when you have the time and commitment to see it through.

Only if you commit fully.

The Mechanics Paradox

Let me bring this full circle to the obsession with mechanics.

Here's the paradox that most players never grasp. Perfect mechanics mean nothing if they don't help you hit the ball hard in competition. You could have an ideal hand position, perfect hip-shoulder separation, optimal weight shift, and textbook bat path.

If you can't time varied speeds, adjust to different locations, make contact under pressure, or hit the ball hard consistently, your mechanics are just pretty positions.

The Kyle Schwarber Reminder

Remember the data from the beginning?

95+ mph exit velocity = higher production. Under 85 mph exit velocity = more outs.

Your mechanics should serve one purpose: putting you in position to hit the ball hard and often.

If your mechanics don't accomplish that, then one of three things is true. Your mechanics are wrong for your body (system doesn't fit), your timing is off (mechanics are fine, timing is the issue), your path needs work (alignment is the problem), or some combination of all three.

The 1,728 Combinations Reminder

You have at least 1,728 potential mechanical combinations. Only ONE is optimal for your body, your timing, your natural movement patterns.

If you're being processed through a system, there's a good chance you're not in your optimal combination, that might be exactly why you're struggling.

The Final Truth

Mechanics are the vehicle. Hitting is the destination.

You can have the most beautiful, mechanically perfect vehicle in the world, however if the engine doesn't fit, the driver doesn't know how to drive it, or the roads require a different vehicle, you're not getting to the destination.

The goal isn't mechanical perfection. The goal is hitting the ball hard consistently in competition. Sometimes that requires a correction. Sometimes that requires compensation. Sometimes that requires throwing out the system and finding your natural combination. It always requires honesty about what's actually working and what's not.

The Three Paths Forward

Path 1: Keep Obsessing Over Mechanics. Chase perfect positions, drill endlessly on movements, hope it translates to games, wonder why it doesn't.

Path 2: Ignore Mechanics Completely. Just "see ball, hit ball," hope talent carries you, get exposed at the next level, hit a ceiling you can't explain.

Path 3: Strategic Mechanics. Understand your natural combination, identify corrections vs. compensations, time your changes with open windows, commit fully to your chosen path, and measure results by hard contact, not pretty positions.

Only one path leads to your potential.

Your Next Step

Are my mechanics serving my hitting, or is my hitting serving my mechanics?

If you're changing your approach, your timing, your aggression to accommodate mechanical positions that feel unnatural, your mechanics are serving themselves, not you. That's a prison, not a platform.

CHAPTER 7

THE ART OF HUNTING PITCHES

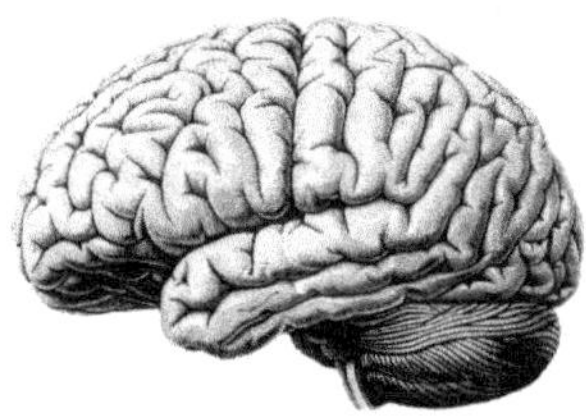

Less Than Two Strikes

"Not swinging has just as much value as swinging when you are hunting speed and location with less than two strikes" - Coaching Wisdom

THE TWO LINEUPS

Spring 2021. I'm talking to J.T. D'Amico right before a University of Washington game when he says something that changes how I think about hitting forever. "We're waiting to see who the opponent puts in the circle," he tells me. "After they make their decision, we'll turn in one of two prepared lineups."

I lean in closer.

"If they throw the X ball pitcher, we turn in lineup A. If it's the Y ball pitcher, lineup B." "What's the difference?" I ask. "Both lineups included a different player. Lineup A has the player with better barrel positioning for pitch X location. Lineup B has the player with better barrel position for pitch Y."

The Problem

Two talented infielders in a top program. Both are good players. Both capable of starting at a top program. Neither could hit the entire strike zone. One dominated pitch X. One dominated Z. When they faced a pitcher who lived in their cold zone, they shared bench time.

Common sense tells you that players should address their weaknesses before advancing to the next level. Here's the uncomfortable reality. Neither of these players was best prepared for their teammate. Coaches understand the competition between pitcher and hitter is all about matchups. In this case, the matchup determined who played and who watched.

The Truth

That conversation was a game changer for me. It revealed how, when, and what methods should be used to assist a player in reducing vulnerabilities within their swing. Giving players the opportunity to maximize their playing time and reduce vulnerabilities to teammates and pitchers.

Fortunately, or unfortunately, for those two young ladies, they had strike zone vulnerabilities. It was apparent they lacked the path capability of getting to areas in the strike zone opposite of their strengths. Path incapable. Not mentally unprepared. Not lacking discipline. Their bodies couldn't get the barrel there.

So every time you hear coaches say "do what you do," remember this: it's what you can't do that will sit you on the bench or hinder your offensive production.

The Origin Of The Problem

The origin of the problem likely started with a phrase you've heard a thousand times. "Hunt your pitch." Another highly talked about, low-taught concept. The problem with "hunt your pitch" is it's a limitation to what you do well. The very thing that may limit your exposure and production.

For coaches who have the eye to identify the hole in your swing, plus a pitcher on the mound who can locate, you're in for a long day. Now you're in a situation where you hope the best pitcher you've ever faced will miss where you do well. Hope is not a strategy.

What if there was a different approach?

ACTING VS. REACTING

What Google Says

Here's what Google says about acting versus reacting.

Acting: Intentional & Deliberate (actions stem from a decision to move forward, make a plan, or achieve a goal). Thoughtful (involves thinking, evaluating, and choosing a response that works best for you). Empowering (puts you in the driver's seat, giving you control over your behavior and feelings).

Reacting: Automatic & Unthinking (immediate responses triggered by emotions, often without much thought). Passive & Dependent (your behavior is influenced by what others say or do, making you feel like you're "along for the ride"). Emotional (based on an emotional interpretation rather than a calm, rational one).

The Problem

Most hitters are reactors. They step in the box with vague intentions: "Be aggressive," "See it and hit it," "Just compete," "Be yourself," "Anything close." Then the pitcher starts mixing speeds and locations. The drop ball at 67 mph with 6" of vertical break. The rise at 64 mph with 5" of vertical break. The changeup at 55 mph with 5" of vertical break. That's up to 11" of vertical separation and 12 mph of speed differential.

Good luck with the "I am tougher than you" and "I am the best right here" mindset. This is hitting, not boxing. You don't just muscle up and make things happen.

You're reacting, automatic, unthinking, along for the ride. The pitcher is acting, intentional, deliberate, in control. Guess who wins?

Think of it like this: you're playing chess, yet you're using a checkers strategy. Every move is reactive. You respond to what your opponent does instead of executing a plan that forces them to respond to you. You're always one step behind.

The Truth

In terms of hitting, most batters would rather be in position to swing with intent, based on the pitcher's evaluation, to empower them to be on time with their rotation and in the right position with the barrel. Achieving the goal of timing and position is the desired outcome and provides an opportunity to maximize bat-to-ball contact.

As it relates to reacting: approaching pitchers who have the ability to change speed and location, along with deception, can make your task harder than it should be. An automatic approach with no preparation for varying your timing and positioning of the barrel puts the authority in the hands of the pitcher or pitch caller.

You can further add layers to the pitcher's advantage by applying methods or biases from others that don't pair up with your thought process or movement patterns. "Just go up there and compete, and know you are the best."

I wish improving at-bat performance came down to motivational speeches, or 30 year old cliches. Unfortunately, it doesn't.

The Great Hitter Myth

Your best players possibly do a phenomenal job of reacting. In reality, they also don't face the best pitchers and pitch callers every day either. How often have you seen "one of the best" transition to college and they struggle?

My theory is: when great pitching and pitch calling meets up with a great swing, I'm betting on the pitcher. Why? Since the pitcher is acting and the swinger is reacting. The actor has the advantage over the reactor.

What if you could flip the script? Acting vs Acting = More action for the hitter.

GAINING THE ADVANTAGE

The Arsenal

When you look at most college and high school pitchers (baseball and softball), they have three pitches. Those pitches are located in specific areas. They have specific speeds, both radar and effective velocities. If you understand this, you can now move your mindset from one of reacting to one of acting.

Think of the strike zone like a battlefield. The pitcher has weapons (pitches). If you study their arsenal, what they throw, where they locate, what speeds, you can position yourself strategically instead of reacting defensively. You become the hunter instead of the hunted.

The Pitch Planning Matrix

Here's the framework that transforms you from reactor to actor.

When you have this mapped for every pitcher you face, you're no longer guessing. You're executing a plan.

Table 7.0 - Pitch Plan Matrix

Pitch Type	Location	Speed	Effective Velocity	My Timing	My Barrel Position
Fastball	Up-In	68 mph	72 mph (EV)	Early start	Flat / parallel
Drop	Down-Away	65 mph	61 mph (EV)	Late start	Steep / angled
Rise	Up-Away	64 mph	64 mph (EV)	On time	Flat / parallel
Change	Down-Middle	58 mph	59 mph (EV)	Latest start	Steep / angled

The Problem

Most players have no idea how to create this matrix for themselves. They hear "hunt your pitch", but don't understand what their timing triggers are, how barrel position changes by location, when to start for different speeds, or how to practice this intentionally.

They take 100 swings in the cage down the middle at the same speed. Then they step in the box and wonder why they can't adjust to the pitcher moving the ball around. You're practicing reaction, not action.

The Truth

Let me break down what you actually need to understand to become a hunter instead of a reactor. First, you possess the primary decision-making capability, not the pitcher. You determine when you start. This is where you need to ensure you understand where your timing issue is.

Timing Elements. When you load, when you shift forward, when you make a swing decision, when you get the foot or heel down, when you decide to rotate. These elements will determine if your barrel is on time, late or early for the pitch.

You don't need to master all of this. Now, as someone trying to improve hitters, I need to understand how you time. Not to be confused with telling you, "be on time". From now on, when you hear, "be on time," you will think or ask, "what timing element."

Telling players how to time is territory I avoid, for fear of being wrong. Helping players understand how they time, now that is a must! If you're late for any one of the timing elements, you sacrifice some of the desired outcome, maximizing ball exit speed. Once you understand your methods of timing, you've entered territory most have never discovered.

THE FAVORITE QUESTION

Ask a player when they start. Next, ask what they call the start. You may discover players have no problem answering both. Now ask when they shift or move forward after loading. Did you discover the response was delayed, if they had one?

I just shared with you my favorite question. If you don't know when you start, how can you maximize your success hunting a variety of speeds and locations if each requires a different start time?

Once there's clarity with your start time, you can pair your start time up with a location and speed. Early timing for inside or faster. Late timing for outside or slower. What you may find, players are using the same trigger to start on every pitcher and every speed. They are missing one of the key elements to hunting speed and location.

My dad would always say, if you are on time, you are late. He was teaching hitting and did not know it. If you are on time for the change up right down the middle, what is your timing for a straight fastball in the same location? No answer is required. Just know the answer if you want to be a hitter!

Now you're halfway there.

THE SECOND HALF: BARREL POSITION

The prioritization of barrel position is predicated upon the height of the pitch. For pitches located at the top of the zone, will produce a barrel that is more parallel to the ground, most players refer to this as flat. Pitches at the bottom of the zone will produce a steeper barrel position coming through the zone.

Think of it like shooting a basketball. You don't use the same arc for a layup and a three-pointer. The target height changes your approach angle. Same with hitting.

When you develop or identify the body timing and barrel position methods, you have just equipped yourself with tools most never discover.

MiLB ROW 1 RESEARCH

I'm sitting in row one at a Mississippi Braves game when I decide to do something that makes everyone around me think I've lost my mind.

Summer 2022. Braves versus Biloxi Shuckers. Both Double-A affiliates. I came to take a break from softball, but I can't turn off the lens. I'm watching how batters are getting out. How they're missing. Whether they're sitting on the pitch that beat them. Whether they adjust. I'm not just watching, I'm assessing.

Attendance was low. I positioned myself directly behind the on-deck circle.

Then I started asking questions.

As players approached the circle, I'd ask: *"What are you sitting on right here?"*

After all, these are professionals. Surely, they're all hunting a specific speed or location.

The looks I received told me everything. Most players didn't know how to answer. Some ignored me entirely. One guy laughed like I'd asked him what color the sky was.

Then number 28 stepped into the circle.

The Conversation

28 had an interesting swing. I took out my phone and recorded his at-bat. He flew out to right field on a changeup.

When he returned to the on-deck circle for his second at-bat, I asked again.

"28, what are you sitting on right here?"

He turned around. Smiled. Looked back at the pitcher. Then back at me.

"Changeup."

First changeup thrown. Crushed!

Third at-bat. "What you got this time?"

No hesitation. "Slider."

First slider? Drove it.

Fourth at-bat. "What you got?"

"Fastball. He's wild and not locating."

Decision. **Discipline**. **Damage**. The Three Pillars, executed pitch by pitch, right in front of me.

But here's what made my jaw drop.

The Reveal

28 wasn't just some Double-A player grinding through the minors.

28 was Corey Ray, first-round pick, fifth overall, 2016 MLB Draft.

After the game, Corey walked over. I had to know.

"When did you start sitting on speed and location?"

"A few weeks ago."

"What changed?"

He told me he'd been studying his swing, looking for what was broken. What he discovered? Nothing was wrong with his swing. The problem was pitch selection. He'd been reacting his entire career. A few weeks earlier, he started hunting.

He mentioned timing. Rhythm. Intention.

Know what he didn't mention? Mechanics.

The Problem

Here's what haunts me about that day. I asked multiple professional baseball players, guys getting paid to hit, what they were sitting on. Most of them couldn't answer. Or wouldn't. Or looked at me like the question made no sense.

These were professionals. And some may have been reacting.

If Double-A players don't have a plan, what makes you think your high school or travel ball player does?

The Truth

A first-round pick. Fifth overall. Years of development at the highest levels of professional baseball. And his breakthrough came from realizing his swing wasn't the problem.

His decisions were.

He stopped reacting. He started hunting. He sat on speed. He sat on location. He executed when he got his pitch.

The question isn't whether this works. Corey Ray proved it works at the professional level. The question is whether you're willing to do what most players, even professionals won't.

Are you a hunter? Or are you one of the guys who would have looked at me like I was an idiot?

You should also consider; do you have the same talent as a first-round pick? Can you even make it near his level without hunting?

CHALLENGE #1: THE TIMING DISCOVERY

This week, answer these questions about YOUR timing.

Part 1: Identify Your Timing Triggers.

What do you call your load?

When do you start your load?

When do you shift forward?

When does your front foot land?

When do you commit to rotation?

Part 2: Test Your Timing. In the cage, have someone throw:

10 pitches inside (note when you started)

10 pitches outside (note when you started)

10 pitches fast (note when you started)

10 pitches slow (note when you started).

Part 3: Analyze. Answer these questions:

Did your start time change based on location?

Did your start time change based on speed?

Were you consciously controlling your start, or was it automatic?

Can you articulate HOW you time pitches?

If you can't answer these questions, you're reacting, not acting. Now, what if you don't have information on the pitcher?

GAME PLANNING WITHOUT INFORMATION

The No-Excuse Approach

For situations where you don't have information on a pitcher, you should do three things.

1. Identify where the catcher is receiving frequently: Up or down, in or out.

2. Get your rhythm each pitch in the dugout: Don't stand still in the dugout, practice your timing trigger.

3. While in the hole, pick your body timing and bat position: What speed will you hunt? What location will you hunt? Where will your barrel be positioned?

The Problem

Most players treat the on-deck circle like a waiting room. They take a few swings. They stretch. They watch their teammate hit. They think about anything except what they're going to do when it's their turn. Then they step in the box with zero plan. Zero intention. Zero advantage. All since this has been Zero teaching.

You're reacting before the pitcher even throws.

You are the number seven batter. There is an average of 4 pitches per batter thrown. You had 24 pitches to get in sync with the pitcher. Now you are going to start on deck and give yourself only 4.

The Truth

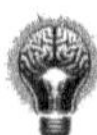

Even without scouting information, you can act instead of reacting by making a timing decision, selecting a barrel position, and choosing your hunt. Think of it like a boxer entering the ring without having watched tape on their opponent. They can still watch the opponent's stance, test with jabs, and adjust based on early reads. You're gathering intelligence in real time and adjusting your strategy.

What if you DO have information?

GAME PLANNING WITH PITCHER INFORMATION

The Subscription Era

For coaches who take the time to identify individual needs to arrive at spots and speeds within the strike zone, understand the value of coupling batter information with pitcher information. With the advent of subscription-based products, pitchers and hitters can no longer hide. They're both in plain sight.

Today, more than ever, players who are developed to sit on speed and location can have the advantage over pitchers. Pitchers do what they do. These available tools allow coaches to identify what pitchers throw, how often they go to locations, the speed of pitches, spin rate, sequencing tendencies, and vertical & horizontal breaks.

Some programs have invested in pitching machines that can simulate speed and location of what's expected from the pitcher. Some machines also consider spin rate to increase the reality of what's expected in the game.

The "We Don't Have Those Machine" Excuse

I know what you're saying: "We don't have this type of equipment. Our program doesn't even have a machine." Well, why not determine what your front-toss speed and distance equivalence is to your playing distance? Why not pitch intentionally to certain areas to identify path possibilities based on what is expected by the pitcher? Ever thought about getting your average front toss distance and speed equivalence to simulate a hitter's game reactionary time?

I'm not allowing you to make that excuse. Where there is a will, there is a way.

I only pull out my pitching machine 10% of the time. It's not required to develop the individual's ability to time the body and position the barrel. Velocity training has a lot of value. However, there are times it can be very damaging.

"Every player has an internal hitting watch, but very few can tell time!" - Rogerick Thompson

The Summer Of 2025

The summer of 2025, I worked with 11 college players and rarely brought out the machine. These players ranged from JUCO to Power 4. One of those players, Lana Johnson batted in the four hole of the WCWS. Machine work was the least of our concerns.

What mattered? Holding players accountable to be disciplined to the plan, hunt specific speeds and locations, practice timing variations, and position the barrel intentionally. You don't need fancy equipment. You need intentional practice.

The Hunter vs. The Sniper

During a session with a student, I was explaining game planning. What I didn't realize was that the student was interpreting "game planning" as just having information on pitchers, what she throws, where she locates, and the speed. There's one other element: understanding the shape of the pitch.

"It is one thing to understand the pitch, though the best preparation is giving players the feel of the shape."
- Chris Malveaux

This information is valuable for players who are not just hunters but snipers. Think about the difference.

> The Hunter sits on a pitch, prepared for a general area.
>
> The Sniper sits speed, location, AND shape, with one timing.
>
> Most players need to become hunters first. Snipers come later. They are rare.

The Problem

Most players try to skip becoming a hunter and try to become snipers immediately. They're too specific. They're hunting fastball up-and-in with cut, and the pitcher throws a fastball up-and-in with run. They take it.

They've narrowed their focus so much that they become passive when anything slightly different appears. Or worse, they become reactors again, waiting for the "perfect" pitch that never comes.

The Truth

Start as a hunter. Master speed and location, then evolve into a sniper. Think of it like learning to shoot a basketball. First, you learn to hit open shots from anywhere. Then you develop your spots, the exact locations where you're deadly. You can't be a sniper if you haven't mastered being a hunter.

CHALLENGE #2: THE GAME PLANNING EXERCISE

For your next opponent, create your own game plan.

Step 1: Gather Intelligence.

What are their primary pitches?

What speeds do they throw?

What are their favorite locations?

What sequences do they use?

Step 2: Create Your Matrix.

Step 3: Practice Your Plan.

Simulate each scenario in practice

Hold yourself accountable to discipline

Table 7.1 – Pitch Game Plan

PITCH TYPE	LOCATION	SPEED	MY TIMING	MY BARREL POSITION
Fastball	Up-In	68 mph	Early start	Flat
Drop	Down-Away	65 mph	Late start	Steep
Change	Down-Middle	58 mph	Latest start	Steep

No swings outside your hunt zones.

Step 4: Execute and adjust.

Did your plan work?

What adjustments did you make?

What would you change next time?

If you don't go through this process, you're guessing, not hunting. What happens when your body can't execute the plan?

CORRECTIVES VS. COMPENSATIONS

The Two Paths

Corrections and compensations are both designed to provide you with opportunities for challenges associated with locations and speeds when you have the capability to sit on speed and location. They're both answers to achieve desired outcomes. The application of either is based on the problem, the time available, and your commitment to create acceptance and repeatability. They're fundamentally different approaches.

The Correction Path

The desired method of improving your performance is addressing the source of undesirable outcomes. This is normally treated in the form of a correction. In pursuit of beneficial change, you could be transitioning from a feeling of comfort to uncomfortable, and vice versa.

Think back to Chapter 6: corrections happen in the off-season when the window is open. There's a time when the window of opportunity to identify your corrections will close. In most cases, this should occur sometime prior to the beginning of the season. Identification of correctives is only part of it; understanding and consistent application are essential.

At this time, you and your instructor must be very efficient with your time and eliminate distractions. In most cases, distractions may be the bat and the ball. These correctives may result in a change in your stance, load, feel, thought, or sight.

The Commitment Requirement

Once the corrective has been identified, you must make a commitment prior to achieving that high level of repeatability. This is where deliberate practice is required, high repetition where there is maximum focus, minimum thought, and ability to demonstrate consistency in a stressful environment.

If the corrective disappears in a controlled stressful environment, what do you think will occur if the stands are full, down by one run, bottom of the seventh? It disappears completely.

The Six Questions

When the off-season is nearing an end, you must answer six questions:

1. Is the proper correction identified?

2. Do you trust the corrective?

3. Will you make the necessary sacrifices to continue the intentional work?

4. Will you communicate with your coach with clarity about what has been discovered?

5. Can you communicate with your coach with clarity to avoid any misunderstandings?

6. Are your coach and instructor able to compare notes to ensure you are not confused?

If there's a lack of trust, proceed to the next step. If there will be no sacrifices to continue intentional work, proceed to the next step. If your coach doesn't understand your corrections, there could be conflict between what has been discovered and what is being directed. Proceed to the next step.

The Problem

Most players get stuck in correction limbo. They identify what needs to change. They work on it for a few weeks. It feels uncomfortable. It doesn't translate immediately. So they half-commit, keep switching between old and new, hope it clicks by opening day, and panic when it doesn't.

Then the season starts, and they're neither corrected nor compensated. They're in no-man's land.

The Truth

The player who becomes the best version of themselves is one who has their A mechanics and their A approach. However, movement is not essential for offensive production, yet it may be essential for power maximization.

You have a few weeks before returning to school or before the season starts. You find yourself still inconsistent with the repeatability of the corrections. Now what? It's time for the second path...

THE COMPENSATION SOLUTION

The Art Of Cheating

I like to refer to compensation as cheating. While watching the road to the 2024 WCWS Super Regionals, I noticed a player I'd studied for a few years do something different. As soon as she stepped in the box, I said: "Wait, she doesn't do that! She's giving herself a chance in the zone to be where she doesn't typically move well."

This was a clear execution of FIO (Figuring It Out). This was an answer. Just not a corrective move answer.

When To Compensate

When you find yourself in a conference series, the last tournament of the year, state championship, playing in front of the college coach, needing to get that run in to advance to the next round, in the last month of your career, at risk of losing your position, or the Women's College World Series, you'll find in a lot of cases that movement correctives are not the correct thing to focus on. A compensation is your go-to.

The Corey Dickerson Story

Corey Dickerson, eleven-year MLB veteran, shared with me a game-time decision. While watching Mike Trout in pregame warm-up, Trout appeared to have his top hand in a specific position at contact. Corey applied in-game what he witnessed just a few hours earlier.

Let that sink in. An eleven-year MLB veteran made a compensation during the game based on something he saw in warm-ups. No week before practice. Not 1000 repetitions. No corrective window. Just adaptation in the moment.

Makes me wonder. Is elite 90% neck up?

The Comfort Challenge

Applying uncomfortable or unfamiliar positions requires a different level of mental toughness or mindset, committing to an uncomfortable position or thought to achieve the desired outcome. If you have any experience with anything, you understand the influence of comfort.

Try this yourself:

Cross your arms right over left, now cross left over right.

Put your pants on the right leg first, now the left leg.

How does that feel? If that simple task required some thought, it may be a great idea to start identifying compensations for vulnerable areas within the strike zone prior to the season.

The Injury Application

When you have a clear understanding of when and how your body gets the barrel to a specific spot, adaptation of compensations during minor injury is a valuable tool. If the body makes a rotational move attempting to square up the ball, from foot down to releasing of the barrel with the wrist, any minor injury can impact the path or power.

Injury can be a huge problem, and not due to potential power production, it gives your teammates a great opportunity to replace you. With the understanding of barrel time and place, you're positioned to expedite the most practical compensations.

The Problem

Most players refuse to compensate as they see it as "giving up" on the correction. They think *I should be able to do this the right way.* Compensation is admitting failure." So they stick with the correction that isn't working. They struggle through games. Their production drops. Their confidence erodes. They lose their spot.

Meanwhile, the player who was willing to compensate, they're producing, they're contributing, and they're playing.

The Truth

Compensation isn't failure. It's a strategy. The two players from the beginning of this chapter? One could have learned to compensate for pitch Z. Open stance. Adjusted timing. Altered barrel position.

Would it have been pretty? No. Would it have kept her in the lineup? Maybe.

Instead, she sat and hoped the coach would choose the pitcher who would throw pitch X. Hope is not a strategy.

THE HUNTER'S MINDSET

Pulling It All Together

You now understand the value of:

Acting vs. reacting (control vs. response)

Timing elements (when you start and move)

Barrel positioning (flat for up, steep for down)

Game planning (with and without information)

Hunter vs. sniper (general vs. specific)

Corrections vs. compensations (fix vs. adapt).

The Ultimate Questions

Am I a hunter or prey? Be honest. Look at your last five at-bats.

Did you have a plan before each pitch?

Did you know what speed and location you were hunting?

Did you adjust your timing and barrel position based on that plan? Or did you step in with vague intentions, see what the pitcher gave you, react to each pitch, and hope for something you could handle?

Your answer reveals everything.

CHALLENGE #3: THE HUNTER'S TRANSFORMATION

For your next game, commit to being a hunter, not a reactor.

Pre-Game:

- Study the pitcher (if available)
- Create your pitch planning matrix
- Identify your primary hunt (speed + location)
- Determine timing and barrel position for each scenario.

Dugout:

- Maintain your rhythm every pitch
- Visualize your timing trigger
- Stay in your body, not your head.

On-Deck:

- Pick your hunt for the first pitch
- Rehearse your timing
- Position your barrel mentally.

At-Bat:

- Execute your plan
- Be disciplined to your hunt
- Make adjustments between pitches

Post-At-Bat:

- Did you hunt or react?
- What adjustments will you make next at-bat?
- Did your plan work?

After three games, evaluate:

- Did being a hunter improve your performance?
- Were you more confident with a plan?
- Did you make better swing decisions?
- Would you ever go back to reacting?

The answer to that last question determines your ceiling as a hitter.

The Two Players Revisited

Remember the two players who couldn't hit the entire strike zone? Here's what they could have done differently.

Player A (Strong X, Weak Y):

Could have worked corrections in the off-season to improve for Y.

Could have compensated in-season with stance adjustments Y as well.

Could have become a threat for both Y and X.

Maybe, she did neither. She hoped their strength would be enough. She hoped the coach would play them against the right pitcher. She hoped her teammate wouldn't perform better. Hope is not a strategy.

One day, they looked up at the lineup card and saw the other player's name where theirs used to

The Choice

You're either going to be the player who hunts:

- Acts with intention
- Has a plan for every pitcher
- Adjusts timing and position deliberately
- Corrects weaknesses or compensates strategically
- Forces pitchers to beat with strategic pitching

Or the player who reacts:

- Waits to see what happens
- Hopes for a "good pitch,"
- Relies on talent and feel
- Ignores weaknesses until benched
- Let pitchers dictate the at-bat.

One player plays. One player watches. Which one are you?

The Final Truth

Let me leave you with this. Great pitching and pitch calling beats great hitting when the hitter is reacting. Great hunting can beat great pitching when the hitter is acting.

The difference isn't talent. It's not even preparation. It's the mindset.

Are you the hunter or the hunted? Do you dictate the at-bat or does the pitcher? Do you have a plan, or do you have hope? Your answer determines whether you're in the lineup or on the bench.

You've just learned the art of hunting pitches. You understand acting versus reacting. You know how to game plan with and without information. You've discovered the difference between hunters and snipers.

Here's the question that's about to blow your mind: What if the zone you're hunting isn't the zone where you're most dangerous?

Right now, you probably think "discipline" means swinging at strikes and taking balls. You've been told your entire career to "stay in the zone." You've been taught that swinging at pitches off the plate is "undisciplined."

What if that's completely wrong for you? What if there are pitches outside the strike zone where you produce better contact than pitches inside the strike zone? What if your hitting zone and the strike zone aren't the same thing? What if the "discipline" you've been taught is actually a prison that's limiting your production?

In the next chapter, you're going to discover the strike zone prison you didn't know you were in. You're going to learn why Luis Arraez hits .404 in a zone that's technically a ball. You're going to understand why Alana Johnson almost destroyed her greatest weapon by shrinking her zone. You're going to face a choice that will determine whether you conform to what coaches say is "right" or break free to what actually produces results.

This chapter will challenge every assumption you have about discipline, the strike zone, and what makes a "good pitch to hit." When you finish it, you'll never look at the strike zone the same way again.

Some of you will choose to stay in the prison given that it's safer. Others will choose to break free. The ones who break free? They become dangerous.

CHAPTER 8

DISCIPLINE AND EXPANDING YOUR ZONE

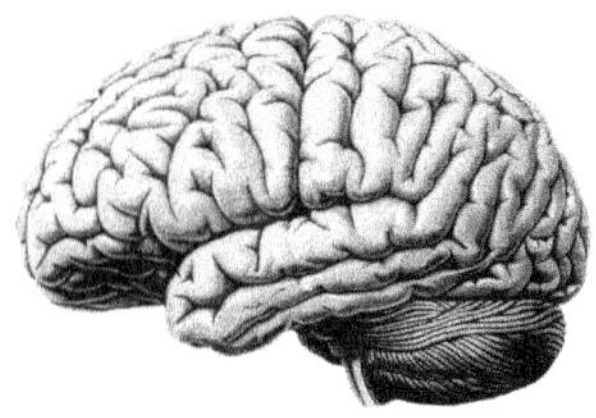

Why All Strikes Are Not Made Equal

"You're in prison, and you don't even know it."
- Coaching Wisdom

THE MOMENT IT ALL DISAPPEARS

You've done everything right. You spent hours in the cage understanding timing and path. You gathered accurate data on the pitcher. You game-planned for who's in the circle. You developed your approach. You know exactly what you're hunting. You step into the batter's box with complete clarity. Then you vacate everything.

The pitcher starts working. Your plan disappears. Your discipline evaporates. Your approach becomes a distant memory. You're swinging at everything or nothing, with no rhyme or reason. Sound familiar?

THAT TALENTED ONE

Before you continue review:

Table 8.0 - Strike zone vs Hitting zone

Zone	Strike?	Your BA	Exit Velo	Swing Decision
Middle-Middle	YES	.350	92 mph	GREEN LIGHT
Down-In	YES	.180	78 mph	RED LIGHT (<2 strikes)
Down-Out (ball)	NO	.425	95 mph	GREEN LIGHT (if timing allows)
Up-In	YES	.150	72 mph	RED LIGHT (<2 strikes)

THE UNCOMFORTABLE QUESTIONS

Now look at your completed table and answer these questions honestly:

Question 1: The Game-Winning At-Bat

SCENARIO: Bottom of the 7th inning. Down by 1 run. Runner on second base. Two outs. The on-deck hitter is 0-for-3 and clearly doesn't have it today. You're the batter.

THE PITCH: Down-and-away, 2 inches off the plate (a ball). According to YOUR data above, this is your .425 zone with 78 mph softball exit velocity.

THE QUESTION: Would you swing at it? If YES: Why do you swing at "balls" in the biggest moment but take them in the 3rd inning?

If NO: Why would you take your BEST pitch (statistically proven) just as an umpire calls it a ball?

Question 2: The Strike Zone Prison

Look at the DOWN-IN zone (a strike) vs. the DOWN-OUT zone (a ball) in your table.

The Math:

Down-In (strike): .180 BA, 63 mph exit velo, 15% hard contact.

Down-Out (ball): .425 BA, 75 mph exit velo, 75% hard contact.

THE QUESTION: Why are you swinging at the strike that produces .180 and taking the ball that produces .425?

FOLLOW-UP: Who benefits from you staying "disciplined" to the strike zone? You or the pitcher.

Question 3: The Talent Waste Calculation

Count how many times last season you:

Swung at strikes in your RED LIGHT zones = _______ times.

Took balls in your GREEN LIGHT zones = _______ times.

Made weak contact on specific strikes = _______ times.

Wished you'd swung at that pitch just off the plate = _______ times.

THE QUESTION: How much production did you leave on the field by being "disciplined" to the strike zone instead of your hitting zone?

Question 4: The Coach's Dilemma

FOR COACHES: You're calling pitches against the hitter described in Table 8.0 above.

You discover: They crush balls down-and-out (.425 BA, 95 mph exit velo).

They're weak on strikes down-and-in (.180 BA, 78 mph exit velo). They've been taught to "swing at strikes and take balls."

THE QUESTION: What's your pitching strategy?

Attack down-in (their weakness)

Avoid down-out (their strength)

Or something else (explain): __________________.

FOLLOW-UP: If you'd attack their weakness and avoid their strength, why do you coach hitters to ignore their strengths just as they're balls?

THE PROBLEM

It doesn't matter how much preparation you've done if you abandon it the moment the game starts. You're a general who spent weeks developing the perfect battle strategy. You studied the enemy. You positioned your troops. You prepared for every scenario. Then the battle begins, and you forget the entire plan. You just react. That's what most hitters do. They prepare like champions and compete like amateurs. Before we dive into discipline, there's a major piece of clarity that is ESSENTIAL.

THE FILTHY PITCHER REALITY

When Discipline Looks Like Failure

You must be honest when facing pitchers that are filthy, what Perry calls effective velocity. This is when pitchers have 2-3 pitches that are tunneled with effective velocity differentials up to 16 miles per hour: At least 8 mph between the slowest and medium pitch, and at least 8 mph between the medium and highest pitch. Honestly, you should be excited that most pitchers pitch to mix it up and not use one of two methods. Pitching to your swing vulnerabilities or pitching with effective velocity methods.

Table 8.1 - Effective Velocity Examples

Pitch	Location	Actual Speed	Effective Velocity	Feel Difference
Drop	Down & In	60 mph	60 mph	+0 mph faster
Drop	Down & Away	60 mph	56 mph	-4 mph slower
Rise	Up & In	60 mph	64 mph	+4 mph faster
Rise	Up & Away	60 mph	60 mph	+0 mph faster

The Problem

When you encounter pitchers with this level of effectiveness, people who have no clue will say: "You don't have discipline," "You should make more competitive swings," "You're not being aggressive enough." What they're missing: you were disciplined, and you did swing at what you thought you had planned for. Unfortunately, the pitcher lied to you. You were deceived. Think of it like a magician's trick. You're watching the right hand since that's where the action should be. The trick is happening in the left hand. "Abracadabra!" The pitcher showed you one thing and delivered another.

The ball comes out looking like a fastball middle-in at 68 mph. Your mind processes that information. Your body commits to that timing. The ball is actually a changeup down-and-away at 58 mph with 5" of drop. By the time you realize you've been deceived, you're already swinging.

The Truth

Against truly elite pitchers with tunneling or effective velocity mastery, even perfect discipline can look like poor discipline. This doesn't excuse chasing bad pitches. It does require honesty about what you're facing. Not every swing-and-miss is a discipline failure. Sometimes it's a deception by the pitcher. The question is: how do you fight back? Before we answer that, we need to address a fundamental misunderstanding...

The Strike Zone Prison

For this section, I will respectfully ask you to remove your bias lens, and keep an open mind.

THE DISTINCTION NOBODY MAKES

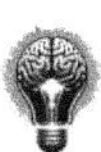

There must be a distinction between the strike zone and the hitting zone. THE STRIKE ZONE: Those nine areas, representing up, middle, down, in, and out. The umpire's domain. Where pitches are called strikes. THE HITTING ZONE: The area where YOU can do damage. Where your timing and path allow you to hit the ball hard. This is an area inside or outside of the strike zone.

The Problem

Most players have been imprisoned to hit only pitches in the strike zone. Unfortunately, many players are confined to an area of minimized production instead of one that has maximum production. You've been put in a box. The power bias. The belief. The barriers you create (or others create for you).

Coaches say:

"Swing at strikes,"

"Stay in the zone,"

"Don't chase,"

"Be disciplined to your zone."

These are extremely valid and valuable. However, it depends:

Are you a good swinger

Are you a hunter

Are you a sniper?

Since, you could be limiting yourself to strikes. You take pitches just off the plate that you could demolish. You confine yourself to an area where your production is actually lower than areas outside the zone. You're in prison, and you don't even know it.

The Truth

What if your best hitting zone isn't the strike zone? What if there are pitches outside the strike zone where you produce better contact, higher exit velocity, and more damage than pitches inside the strike zone? What if the "discipline" you've been taught is actually limiting your production? This is about to blow your mind…

Check the Facts: Luis Arraez of the San Diego Padres had a .292 batting average in 2025 (statcast). Below are his batting averages for each of the 13 zones.

Legend: NS = Not a Strike (outside the strike zone)

Key Insights: Strike Zone vs. Hitting Zone

Highest Batting Averages

Zone 13 (NS-Down/Out) - .404 BA - NOT A STRIKE X

Zone 5 (Mid-Middle) - .366 BA - Strike ✓

Zone 12 (NS-Up/In) - .317 BA - NOT A STRIKE ✗

Table 8.2 - Luis Arraez 2025 Batting Averages by Zone

Zone	Location	Strike Zone?	Batting Average
1	Up-Away	✓ YES	.237
2	Up-Middle	✓ YES	.311
3	Up-In	✓ YES	.143
4	Mid-Away	✓ YES	.288
5	Mid-Middle	✓ YES	.366
6	Mid-In	✓ YES	.275
7	Down-Away	✓ YES	.310
8	Down-Middle	✓ YES	.212
9	Down-In	✓ YES	.325
11	NS-Up/Out	✗ NO	.237
12	NS-Up/In	✗ NO	.317
13	NS-Down/Out	✗ NO	.404
14	NS-Down/In	✗ NO	.245

Lowest Batting Averages

Zone 1 (Up-Away) - .296 BA - Strike ✓

Zone 8 (Down-Middle) - .212 BA - Strike ✓

Zone 3 (Up-In) - .143 BA - Strike ✓

The Discipline Paradox

Comparison:

The Critical Question: Should Luis Arraez:

Be "disciplined" and take Zone 13 pitches (.404 BA)?

Be "aggressive" and swing at Zone 8 pitches (.212 BA)?

Hunt his hitting zone regardless of the umpire's strike zone?

THE ANSWER: Arraez hits nearly 200 points higher on a ball (Zone 13) than on a strike (Zone 8).

THE LESSON: "Discipline" to the strike zone can mean limiting production in your hitting zone.

Note: Other considerations not included: speed ranges and pitch type. Pulling back additional layers may identify the specific pitches he should consider in zone 13. Source: MLB Statcast 2025 Season Data. Application: Use this as a model for your own zone analysis. Your hitting zone may not be the strike zone.

Now, keep your mind open, remove your bias and ask yourself this question. Should he have never swung pitches in zones 12 and 13? Was he more productive here than areas inside of the strike zone? Also, just as all strikes are not made equal, and neither are pitches that come through the zone you are testing. A 55-mph, 65-mph and 72-mph outside curve in zone 9 are not all made equal. Pairing your speed rage with location is essential.

THE HITTING ZONE DISCOVERY

Table 8.3 - The Hitting Zone Discovery

Category	Zone	Strike?	Batting Average
BEST ZONE	13 (Down-Out)	X NO (Ball)	.404
WORST STRIKE ZONE	8 (Down-Middle)	✓ YES (Strike)	.212
DIFFERENCE			+.192

After you've gathered data on yourself in the strike zone, I challenge you to challenge yourself. Make a visit to the cage and set up a tee outside the zone in the four main areas:

Up and in (off the plate),

Down and in (off the plate)

Up and away (off the plate)

Down and away (off the plate)

By the way, why have you not invested in a tee that gets at or below the knee?

After you've taken equal swings in each area, identify your top two areas of best contact. Take some challenging soft tosses in your top two productive areas.

Next, give yourself some game-like speeds off the pitching machine in the best contact area. (Wear protective gear for game-like speeds).

Finally, take some pitches off the machine in your weakest area in the strike zone and your strongest area outside the strike zone.

The Problem

Most players have never done this experiment. Why? Since they've been told their entire career:

"Don't swing at balls"

"Lay off pitches out the zone"

"That's not your pitch"

So they never test whether they can actually hit those pitches. They never discover that their weakest strike might produce worse contact than their strongest ball. They stay in prison since they never tested the walls.

The Truth

> You may discover your strike zone and hitting zone are not made equal. A pitch that's a ball (outside the strike zone) that you crush for line drives might be more valuable than a pitch that's a strike (inside the strike zone) that you roll over for weak ground balls.

If I just created a huge contradiction in your coaching and your capabilities, that is absolutely phenomenal. That's the type of connection I wanted to make. In order for you to be the best version of yourself, these are the types of discussions you need to have with your instructor, coach, or student.

CHALLENGE #1: THE ZONE DISCOVERY EXPERIMENT

This week, run the hitting zone experiment:

PHASE 1: TEE WORK (OUTSIDE THE ZONE) Set up tee in these locations (all outside the strike zone):

Up-and-in (ball)

Up-and-away (ball)

Down-and-in (ball)

Down-and-away (ball).

Take 10 swings in each location. Grade contact quality (A, C or F).

PHASE 2: SOFT TOSS (TOP 2 OUTSIDE ZONES) Take 20 soft tosses in your two best outside-zone areas. Track: exit velocity, ball flight, contact quality.

PHASE 3: GAME SPEED - MACHINE WORK (COMPARISON) Take 10 swings: weakest strike zone area. Take 10 swings: strongest outside-zone area.

Compare: Which produces better contact?

PHASE 4: THE REVELATION Answer these questions:

Did any outside-zone area produce better contact than inside-zone areas?

Were you surprised by your strongest outside-zone area?

Would you swing at those pitches in a game?

Have coaches told you not to swing at those pitches?

If your strongest outside-zone area produces better contact than your weakest inside-zone area, you've been limiting yourself.

If that is too simple for science, just use the numbers…

Fangraph.com Plate zone discipline statistics:

O-Swing% = Swings at pitches outside the zone / pitches outside the zone.

Z-Swing% = Swings at pitches inside the zone / pitches inside the zone. Swing% = Swings / Pitches.

O-Contact% = Number of pitches on which contact was made on pitches outside the zone / Swings on pitches outside the zone.

Z-Contact% = Number of pitches on which contact was made on pitches inside the zone / Swings on pitches inside the zone.

Contact% = Number of pitches on which contact was made / Swings. Zone% = Pitches in the strike zone / Total pitches.

F-Strike% = First pitch strikes / PA. SwStr% = Swings and misses / Total pitches.

It would be fair to understand each hitter by his or her O-Swing% + Z-Contact%. The position of the zone is determined by in, out, up and down. It is essential to have specifics for the zone testing areas. Discovering this creates a problem…

A MUCH-NEEDED DETOUR: THE LANA CONVERSATION

The Summer Of 2024

It was the summer of 2024 when Lana said something that concerned me: "I'm not going to swing at pitches more than a ball off the plate." This was a decision made due to her discipline challenges the previous season. A decision I did not agree with. I'd seen her demolish balls outside of the strike zone from high school through the college Power 5 level. Too many players are put in a box by coaches, and I didn't want Lana to package herself up in one.

The Problem

Lana felt she needed to shrink her hitting zone to improve her discipline. In her mind: Better discipline = better production. Therefore, shrink the zone.

I saw something different. I saw rhythm issues that created a contact issue. My concern, I didn't want her to remove one of the most valuable tools in her toolbox.

After all, she was known for hitting pitches 2-3 balls off the plate over the fence when she was in rhythm and on time, regardless of her position once the foot got down. When she was out of rhythm and off time, it wasn't the location. It was her rhythm impacting her timing. Symptom versus issue. Different perspectives. How do you resolve that?

The Truth: Components Of Athlete Connectivity

1. CONCERN/FEELINGS: Lana was concerned about missed opportunities to improve her offensive contributions to the team.

2. COMMUNICATION: A dialogue between the athlete and the teacher. What I saw and what she felt were two different things, I saw rhythm issues that could lead to a timing solution. She saw discipline issues and felt there should be a zone-shrinking solution. I expressed what she risked giving up. She expressed what she felt. This conversation was at least a thirty-minute dialogue between the two of us.

In my effort to convince Lana not to shrink her hitting zone, I questioned myself. We talk about the importance of communication in relationships, right? Well, isn't player and teacher a relationship? This should not be a delivery and acceptance from me and my players. If hitting is 90% from the neck up, the method of communication should be reciprocated. As a result, understanding how they think and feel, not just how they swing.

The Most Valuable Tool

Communication.

Think about your own relationships with coaches or instructors.

Is it a dialogue or a monologue?

Do you express what you feel, or just accept what's delivered?

Do they understand how you think, or just how you swing?

Communication isn't just speaking, it's listening, understanding, and finding truth together. In Lana's case, we found a solution that didn't require her to shrink her zone. We addressed the rhythm issue, which improved her discipline, which allowed her to keep her greatest weapon and the ability to hit balls off the plate over the fence. What Lana was able to do, is something that can make pitching coaches lose sleep...

WHAT PITCHING COACHES DON'T WANT YOU TO DISCOVER

HOW TO SHIFT THE PLATE

Before You Proceed: The Shift That Changes Everything

CRITICAL WARNING:

What you are about to read may challenge everything you have heard about discipline and approach. Shifting the plate can be defined as chasing.

You've been told your entire career: "Don't chase." What if that advice is keeping you in prison?

The Definition Problem

Here's what the baseball dictionary says:

Chase = Swinging at pitches outside the zone.

STOP AND THINK ABOUT "CHASE": How do you define chase? Is it just limited to swinging at areas outside of the zone? Does it apply to swinging outside of your plan, even when the pitch is in the zone? Can we please get this added to the definition of chase also!

Is it a chase when you are deceived by the pitch? Based on the hitter's abilities, is chase always a bad thing? Should chase also be the equivalent of not discipline. What if you hit some balls better than you hit strikes?

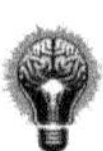 One last thought before returning to the data! You have a player that hits 1-2 balls off the plate very well. Swinging outside of the strike zone is not your preference. Should you at least practice this so when he/she is fooled, they can apply their best chase swing? Do you have any players on your roster that don't chase? What if you taught them how to properly chase?

Yes! Properly chase!

How to respond properly when the body is disobedient to the decision made by the mind? Would this be a better option than staying back, being perfectly balanced, then whiffing?

Revisiting the data: Fangraphs tracks something called "plate discipline statistics." Here's what they measure:

O-Swing% = How often you swing at pitches outside the zone.

O-Contact% = How often you make contact on those outside swings.

Z-Swing% = How often you swing at pitches inside the zone.

Z-Contact% = How often you make contact on those inside swings.

The assumption? High O-Swing% = bad hitter. Go back and look at Luis Arraez's 2025 data again: Let me ask you a simple question: Should Arraez swing at zone 13 or zone 7?

The "correct" answer: Zone 7, since it's a strike.

The smart answer: Zone 13, as he hits .404.

*This decision and outcome could be limited to the pitch type.

The Truth

Once you've confirmed there are areas outside the strike zone where you produce better contact, compare those to areas within the strike zone. You may have just discovered you've been barred from areas of greater production and confined to areas of low production. You've been coached to avoid your strength and attack your weakness.

It is right in front of you and you don't even see it.

How many players have you seen with the long swing? I am talking about those who cast the barrel early or prior to launch.

What about those whose hands move distal from their body, prior to launch?

What pitch do you think they can hit the best? A ball and a half off the plate for a ball or, ball and a half inside for a strike? Here is another one. Why do you tell players to get on the plate or off the plate? Just let that one sink in. You could be in prison, and the strike zone is the cell.

The Shift Concept

Once you've identified your hitting zone assets and strike zone liabilities, you can precisely establish a plan of attack for each pitcher you face.

For players who create better barrel paths above or below the zone, they have the opportunity to shift the zone down vertically.

For players who can time pitches late or early, they have the ability to shift the plate left or right.

These plate shift opportunities could be a liability for a pitcher throughout the lineup in any inning. Think of it like a basketball player with an unorthodox shooting form. Mechanically inefficient. They make shots. Do you fix the form or let them shoot?

The Problem

There are coaches who don't have the time to develop or the skill to address individual needs in a team setting. So, some put everyone in the same box: "Swing at strikes," "Stay in your zone," "Don't chase." It's easier.

It's uniform. It's teachable to 20-35 players at once. It limits the players who could thrive outside the box, or strike zone. You're a talented artist who paints outside the lines. The art teacher keeps telling you to color inside the lines since that's the "right way." Your best work happens outside the lines. Do you conform or do you create?

The Coach's Warning

WARNING: If you apply the out-of-the-zone approach, and your coach is not on board with this, you better be good at it. Here's the reality: most coaches will see O-Swing% go up and assume you lack discipline. They won't see your .404 batting average on those "bad" pitches. They'll see the stat that says you're "chasing" and bench you. This is why communication matters. This is why understanding your coach's philosophy matters. This is why you need data to back up your approach.

The Player's Choice

OPTION 1: Conform to the strike zone, even if it limits your production.

OPTION 2: Expand to your hitting zone and risk your coach's disapproval.

OPTION 3: Communicate with your coach, show them your data, and build your case.

Most players choose Option 1 as it's safe. Elite players choose Option 3 given that it's smart. Which one will you choose?

The Challenge

Before you expand your zone, answer these questions: Do I have data proving I hit certain "balls" better than certain "strikes"? Can I articulate why this expansion helps my production? Is my coach open to individualized approaches? Am I elite enough at this to justify the risk? If you answered "yes" to all four, you're ready to shift the plate. If you answered "no" to any of them, proceed with caution.

The Final Truth

Shifting the plate isn't for everyone. It's for players who:

- Have done the assessment work, have the data to prove it works
- Have the courage to challenge convention
- Have the skill to execute consistently.

If that's you, shift away. If it's not, stay disciplined to the strike zone until you've earned the right to expand.

> Never forget that the strike zone is a starting point, not a prison. Some players thrive inside it. Others break free from it. Which player are you?

IMPORTANT: **This section is not encouraging an undiscipline approach**. It is identifying where swing flaws can make hitting fun. A player or coach must do their homework on a player prior to providing out of the zone green lights. What you'll discover with individual approaches is the challenge you'll create for pitchers. A lineup of variable swings and approaches is a great threat to any pitcher or pitching staff. Why does variability matter so much?

THE VARIABILITY ADVANTAGE

The Pitching Staff Paradox

The average college coach wants variability in their pitching staff. They understand the value of:

Change of speeds

Change of location

Different shapes and movement

When a lineup is having success against a pitcher, what does the coaching staff say? "We need to show them something different." This pitching change could be:

Taking out the drop ball pitcher and putting in a rise ball pitcher,

Going from higher velocity to lower velocity,

Switching from right-handed to left-handed

What would variability of styles throughout a lineup do to the pitching changes?

The Problem

Most lineups are filled with cookie-cutter hitters. They have the same approach, same timing, same swing philosophy, same strengths, same weaknesses. It's easy for pitching coaches to game plan against you.

They can say: "This team is vulnerable up-and-in," "They all chase the drop ball," "Stay away and they can't hurt you." One strategy beats nine hitters.

Think of it like a military strategy. If all your troops use the same tactics, the enemy only needs to prepare one defense. If every soldier uses different tactics, the enemy can't prepare for everything.

The Truth

A lineup of variable swings and approaches forces pitchers to adjust hitter by hitter instead of lineup by lineup. Imagine a pitching coach trying to prepare when:

Hitter 1 crushes high pitches (flat path)

Hitter 2 demolishes low pitches (steep path)

Hitter 3 times early and pulls everything (early timing)

Hitter 4 times late and drives opposite field (disconnects and cast)

Hitter 5 sits on speed and locations

Hitter 6 sees it and hit it.

How does a pitching coach survive this type of lineup? Most can't. You must adjust in real-time. Which means the hitters now have the advantage. How do you implement this in a team environment?

EXPANDING THE STRIKE ZONE IN A TEAM ENVIRONMENT

The Implementation Challenge

What problems would a lineup present to a pitching staff if the lineup had variability in their styles or approaches? Would you rather face a lineup of hitters that all hang back on their back leg and produce positive attack angles, where the sweet spot is at the bottom of the zone? You may be okay with that when you have a pitcher that can locate velocity up and in for a strike. How would you feel if you had a pitcher that could only locate the drop ball down and away for a strike? Now you have a problem.

The Team Implementation Process

It's easier to individualize in a one-on-one session. On the other hand, it can add tremendous value in a team setting.

STEP 1: IDENTIFY STRENGTHS AND WEAKNESSES For each player on the team, identify strengths and weaknesses in the strike zone.

STEP 2: IDENTIFY PLATE SHIFTERS Which players are able to shift the plate (vertically or horizontally)?

STEP 3: EVALUATE VULNERABILITIES The coach evaluates and identifies vulnerable areas within the strike zone. The important piece: identifying the type of vulnerability:

Mechanical

Timing

Discipline.

STEP 4: ASSESS CORRECTION WINDOW Is there a timing window wide enough to consistently apply correctives or compensations prior to the season?

STEP 5: CREATE INDIVIDUALIZED SOLUTIONS (Correctives or Compensations). What you may uncover is a lineup that is difficult for a pitching staff to prepare for.

The Problem

Some coaches resist this approach because:

- It requires individual attention
- It contradicts their systematic philosophy
- It feels chaotic instead of uniform
- It's harder to teach
- It requires flexibility in their thinking
- It requires more time than they have.

So, they keep everyone in the same box and wonder why the best pitchers shut down their entire lineup with one approach. Control (down the middle) feels safer than variability (all edges). Control is predictable. Predictable is exploitable.

The Truth

I'm not a fan of sitting on one pitch, though if you have three players that move well to an elevated pitch, and you have corrections or compensations for the remaining hitters... now that rise ball pitcher has a problem. Since you've just individualized solutions for each of the six individual hitters who can't move well. Think about what this means for a pitching coach:

- They can't just say "attack up,"
- They can't rely on one weapon
- They have to adjust constantly
- They're always uncomfortable

Welcome to what hitters feel every at-bat. Now the tables are turned.

CHALLENGE #2: THE LINEUP VARIABILITY AUDIT

If you're a coach or a player on a team, run this audit:

PART 1: IDENTIFY YOUR LINEUP PATTERNS For your starting nine, answer:

How many hitters are vulnerable up vs. down?

How many hitters time early vs. late?

How many hitters pull vs. go opposite field?

How many hitters swing at strikes only vs. expand the zone?

Are we predictable or variable?

PART 2: IDENTIFY UNTAPPED STRENGTHS For each hitter, answer:

Do they hit any outside-zone areas better than inside-zone areas?

Can they shift the plate vertically or horizontally?

Have we limited them to the strike zone when they could expand?

What's their actual hitting zone vs. their assigned zone?

PART 3: CREATE VARIABILITY Develop a plan:

Which hitters can expand their zone safely?

Which hitters need corrections to improve weak zones?

Which hitters should compensate to utilize outside-zone strengths?

How variable will our lineup be after implementation?

PART 4: TEST AND MEASURE After implementing for three weeks:

Did opposing pitchers struggle more to prepare?

Did our overall production increase?

Did individual hitters thrive with expanded zones?

Would we ever go back to uniform approaches? If you discover your lineup is more effective with variability, you've just learned what pitching coaches already know.

TAKING A PAGE FROM THE PITCHING COACH'S PLAYBOOK

The Arms Race

Some programs can increase their production by taking a page out of pitching coaches' playbooks. Pitching coaches have a variety of arms that produce a variety of pitches. This has a greater opportunity of leveling the playing field when those pitchers have to face a variety of paths and approaches. How do you think it would work if you put players in different compartments instead of the same box?

The Problem

The implementation of variety isn't easy given that the first person it will challenge may be you, the coach/instructor. For those with a growth mindset, it could be a little easier. If your mindset is fixed and you have a belief that players should conform to you and not you to the player, the timing window may not be wide enough to determine the mechanical needs. Think about the coach who says:

- "We do it this way"
- "Everyone needs to look the same"
- "Individual approaches create chaos"
- "Uniformity is strength"

That coach is creating a pitching coach's dream: a predictable lineup. Yes, you may get away with this, until the playoffs. Or when you meet up against that team who has implemented these methods.

Meanwhile, the coach who says:

- "Let's find what works for you"
- "Individual strengths create unpredictability"
- "Variability is our weapon"
- "Flexibility is strength."

That coach is creating a pitching coach's nightmare: an adaptable lineup.

The Truth

A few simple tests identifying strengths and weaknesses, along with reviewing some simple data, could be game-changing. Before the production of the game-changing happens, there may be some changing of the minds required. Think of it like a military general who's always used the same formation. It's worked for years. It's comfortable. It's predictable. Then a new enemy emerges that exploits that formation. Does the general adapt or does he keep losing? The same choice faces coaches. The same choice faces players. Do you conform to the box or do you break free?

THE DISCIPLINE PARADOX

Bringing It Full Circle

Discipline. You thought this chapter was about swinging at strikes and laying off balls. About being patient. About not chasing. It's actually about something completely different. Real discipline isn't about conforming to the strike zone. It's about understanding your hitting zone and hunting within it. Real discipline isn't about taking balls off the plate. It's about knowing which balls off the plate you can crush and which ones you can't. Real discipline isn't about being predictable. It's about being intentionally variable.

The Problem

Most players confuse discipline with conformity:

"Good discipline" = swinging at strikes

"Bad discipline" = swinging at balls

"Disciplined hitter" = patient hitter.

What if a "disciplined hitter" is actually:

Someone who knows their hitting zone (strike zone or not),

Someone who hunts within their zone aggressively

Someone who expands when timing allows

Someone who shifts the plate for an approach

That's a completely different definition of discipline. Think about a sniper. Is the sniper "disciplined" since they wait patiently? Or because they know exactly when to pull the trigger based on conditions? Discipline isn't patience. It's precision.

The Truth

All strikes are not made equal, but all balls aren't made equal either. Some balls (outside the strike zone) are better pitches to swing at than some strikes (inside the strike zone). Your discipline should be to your hitting

zone, not the strike zone. When you understand your hitting zone, your timing capabilities, and your barrel positioning strengths, you can expand or shrink your zone strategically. You're not chasing. You're hunting. You're not being undisciplined. You're being smart. You're not conforming to the strike zone. You're dominating your hitting zone.

The Two Types Of Discipline

TYPE 1: CONFORMIST DISCIPLINE

Swings at strikes only, confined to the strike zone, predictable to pitchers and limited production. Safe but ineffective.

TYPE 2: STRATEGIC DISCIPLINE

Swings within their hitting zone, expands when timing allows, unpredictable to pitchers and maximized production. Aggressive but effective. Which type are you? Don't answer too quickly.

Look at your actual results:

Do you take pitches you could crush given that they're "balls"?

Do you swing at pitches that are "strikes" but produce weak contact?

Have you ever tested your outside-zone production?

Do you know your actual hitting zone?

Your answers reveal your type.

CHALLENGE #3: THE 30-DAY DISCIPLINE TRANSFORMATION

For the next 30 days, commit to strategic discipline:

WEEK 1: DISCOVERY

Run the Zone Discovery Experiment (Challenge #1). Identify your actual hitting zone. Document outside-zone areas where you produce.

WEEK 2: PRACTICE

Spend 50% of cage time in your strongest outside-zone areas. Develop timing and barrel positioning for those areas. Build confidence in your expanded zone.

WEEK 3: SIMULATION

Take game-like at-bats where you hunt your hitting zone (not strike zone). Practice expanding when timing allows. Practice contracting when timing doesn't.

WEEK 4: IMPLEMENTATION

In games, be disciplined to YOUR hitting zone. Swing at balls you can crush. Take strikes you can't. Track production vs. previous approach.

EVALUATION:

After 30 days, answer: Did my production increase with strategic discipline? Was I more confident with my expanded zone? Did pitchers struggle more to beat me? Would I ever go back to conformist discipline? If your answer to the last question is no, you've broken free from the strike zone prison.

Your Choices

You're standing at a choice point right now.

CHOICE 1: STAY IN THE BOX

Conform to the strike zone, swing at strikes, take balls, be predictable, limit production to what coaches say is "right."

CHOICE 2: BREAK FREE

Discover your hitting zone, hunt within your zone (strike zone or not), be unpredictable, maximize production based on what YOUR body can do.

Most players choose Choice 1 since it's safer. It's what coaches want. It's what everyone says is "disciplined." Safe doesn't win championships. Lana almost chose Choice 1. She almost shrunk her zone to "improve discipline." After we had a conversation. After we communicated. We found a better solution. She stayed dangerous.

The two players from Chapter 7? They chose Choice 1. They conformed to what they were told. They stayed in the box, their box without compensation. And they sat on the bench.

The Uncomfortable Truth

Here's what you need to understand as we close this chapter: The best hitters in the world expand and contract their zones based on timing, pitcher, and situation. They're not confined to strikes. They're not "disciplined" in the traditional sense. They're strategic. They know when to hunt a ball up-and-in that's 3 inches off the plate as their timing and barrel can get there. They know when to take a strike middle-middle as they're not on time. They're disciplined to their hitting zone, not the umpire's strike zone. That's what makes them elite.

Your Next Move

1. Have I ever tested my hitting zone outside the strike zone?

2. Do I take pitches I could crush since they're "balls"?

3. Do I swing at pitches that are "strikes" but produce weak contact?

4. Am I confined to the strike zone or am I hunting my hitting zone?

5. Is my discipline conformist or strategic?

Your answers reveal whether you're in prison or free. Only free hitters reach their potential.

You've just discovered that your hitting zone might not be the strike zone. You've learned that all strikes are not equal, and neither are all balls. You understand that discipline isn't conformity to the umpire's zone, it's strategic hunting within your zone. Here's the reality check that's coming: Everything you've learned in the past eight chapters is completely worthless if you don't know how to apply it when it matters most. When does it matter most? College and professionally.

Four years. That's all you get. Four years to prove yourself, maximize your potential, and leave a legacy. No minor leagues. No developmental time. No "I'll figure it out later." Most players waste their first two years as they show up unprepared for realities they didn't anticipate. They show up thinking their high school success matters. It doesn't. It just bought them bench time.

They show up thinking their talent is enough. It isn't. Everyone has talent. They show up thinking the coaches will figure them out. They won't. The coaches have 20+ players and limited time.

In the next chapter, you're going to discover what college coaches wish high school players knew before they arrived on campus. You're going to learn why the players who can articulate their strengths and weaknesses on day one gets opportunities the others don't. You're going to understand the difference between systems of similarity and systems of individuality. You're going to discover how to use the same scouting technology against pitchers that pitching coaches use against you. This chapter is your roadmap for making sure your four years count. Since you don't get a second chance at this.

The players who read this chapter and apply it? They thrive from freshman year. The players who ignore it? They spend their college career wondering why their talent never translated. Which player will you be?

CHAPTER 9

MAXIMIZING YOUR LAST FOUR YEARS

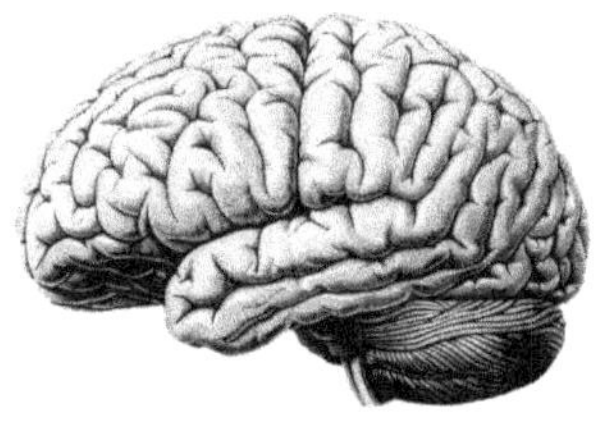

The College Coach Advantage

"After college. No minor leagues. No professional career. No 'I'll figure it out later.' This is it." - Coaching Wisdom

THE DAY YOUR SUCCESS STOPS MATTERING

YOUR BATTING AVERAGE IS A LIE

The .450 Illusion

You walk onto campus with a .450 batting average. Three years of dominance. Tournament MVP awards. Numbers that made college coaches take notice. Here's what nobody told you: Your days of a .450 hitter could be over.

The Reality Check

Some people know the truth. Unfortunately, they can't afford to tell you. It might hurt your feelings or your parents'. In this business, that risk can cost them a client. Good players bring attention. Attention brings more players. That cycle often matters more to them than your growth.

The Problem

Think about the pitching you faced in high school and travel ball:

How many pitches could be located in all four quadrants consistently?

How many pitching coaches were calling pitches based on your swing vulnerabilities?

How many teams had sophisticated scouting reports on you?

How many pitchers had 3+ pitches with effective velocity differentials?

How many pitchers you faced will be best at your college level of play?

The truth? Almost none.

Your .450 average wasn't built on skill against quality competition. It was built on:

INFERIOR PITCH CALLING Most travel ball coaches don't study hitters. They have a generic game plan:

"Throw strikes"

"Mix speeds"

"Work the corners"

They're not watching your: Timing tendencies, barrel path vulnerabilities, swing-and-miss locations, weak contact zones. They're guessing. You're feasting on their guesses.

LIMITED PITCHER SKILL High school and travel ball pitchers are still developing. Most can't consistently locate, command multiple pitches, execute sequences, adjust mid-game based on what's working. When you face a pitcher who can only throw one pitch for strikes, your .450 average means nothing.

NO REAL SCOUTING How many opponents had video of your at-bats from previous tournaments? Detailed scouting reports on your tendencies? Pre-game plans specifically designed to exploit YOUR weaknesses? In college? All of them.

The Truth

That .200 hitter in college. She was always a .200 hitter. She just never faced pitching good enough to expose it. Her high school stats were built on pitchers who couldn't locate, coaches who didn't scout, competition that didn't adjust and weaknesses that were never attacked.

She arrived at college and faced pitchers who can paint corners, coaches who know her holes better than she does, competition that adjusts after one at-bat and systematic attacks on every vulnerability. The pitching got better. Along with the scouting. Now her high school .450 average is a college .180.

THE WAKE-UP CALL

This isn't meant to crush your confidence. It's meant to give you clarity. If you understand why your stats were inflated, you can prepare differently. You can identify your real strengths (not what worked against inferior competition), scout yourself like a college pitching coach would, address weaknesses before they're exploited, and arrive at college prepared for quality pitch calling.

The Questions

"If I faced the best pitcher in my state, with the best pitching coach calling pitches based on my swing vulnerabilities, every single game... what would my batting average be?" "What is my batting average against the top 3 pitchers I faced in tournament ball?" That's your real number.

Not the .450 you hit against pitchers who couldn't locate but one pitch.

Not the .400 you hit when nobody scouted you.

Not the .380 you hit when coaches just said, "throw strikes."

Your real number is what you'd hit when someone is actively trying to exploit you. That number? It's probably 100-200 points lower than what's on your recruiting profile.

The Advantage

The good news is most players don't know this. They show up at college thinking their stats were real. They believe their success was earned against quality competition. They assume their approach will translate. You now know better.

Knowing this gives you a massive advantage:

1. You can prepare for real pitch calling (Chapter 7).

2. You can scout yourself like opponents will (Chapter 5).

3. You can identify actual weaknesses before they're exploited (Chapter 6).

4. You can arrive at college with answers, not just talent (rest of this chapter).

Your batting average was a lie. Some couldn't identify the truth, and others refused to tell you the truth. Now you know the truth.

What will you do with it?

You walk onto campus with a resume that would make anyone proud. You're a high school all-state, travel ball MVP awards, tournament championships, with a scholarship offer in hand. You're ready to dominate. You've earned your spot. You're prepared to show everyone what you can do. Then reality hits you in the face.

Your high school and travel ball success? It just bought you more time on the bench than in the batter's box.

"They are not ready when they step on campus."
- Unnamed College Coach

The Problem

When you walk onto a college campus, everything changes in ways you didn't anticipate. The days are over when you just "see the ball and hit the ball." You now have a pitcher that is as good as you, working with a coach who may have studied you and knows you better than you know yourself.

They've watched your stories and posts. They've charted your tendencies. They've identified your holes. They've built a strategy to exploit every weakness you have. You? You're just showing up hoping your talent shows up too.

The Truth

Hitting the round ball with a round bat in softball and baseball is the same when it comes to the strike zone and the task. Bat materials, balls, and pitch shapes have differences, now once the ball makes it to the desired destination, the task in both sports is equal.

Suggestion, Don't Do This:

When it comes to the softball player, don't compare college softball to the MLB. In most cases, your career is over after college. Even if you play professionally, you'll need to supplement your income.

High-level college baseball players will have the opportunity to advance to the professional level, where baseball becomes their job. They'll experience developmental levels before making it to the show, if they make it. You're forever a "student" athlete. Which means you have four years. That's it. Four years to maximize your potential, prove yourself, and leave a legacy. You are nowhere close to being who you could be! No pressure, right? This is what separates those who thrive from those who survive...

THE ADVANTAGE YOU DIDN'T KNOW YOU NEEDED

Understanding Yourself As A Hitter Early

> Players who walk into college with their answer to a variety of speeds and locations come in with an advantage over their teammates. Coaches would like to coach, but more than anything, they're there to win.

You can't be coached until they can teach you. Guess what, you're not the only one who may not be familiar with their strengths and weaknesses. This puts the most talented and the longest-tenured in position to get the first and most frequent opportunities.

You may say that's not fair. Well, they're trying to win, and you're no longer the best player in your town or state. You could easily go from the best one on the team to the worst on the team in a few weeks. Facts!

The Problem

Most players arrive at college thinking their talent is enough. They assume:

"I'll figure it out as I go,"

"The coaches will tell me what to do"

"My natural ability will translate"

"I just need reps."

The uncomfortable reality is, the coaches don't have all year to figure you out. They have 20-plus hitters on the roster. They have a season to win. They have limited practice time. They have pressure from administration.

You have class to attend, studying to get done, and let's not forget, you will try to have a great time.

> If you can't articulate who you are as a hitter, you're going to get lost in the shuffle.

Think of it like showing up to a new job on your first day. Your boss asks: "What are your strengths? Where do you need support? How do you work best?"

You respond: "I don't know. Just tell me what to do." How long do you think that job lasts?

The Truth: The Three Things You Must Know

There is tremendous benefit in clearly understanding yourself. You may not have all the answers, however there are some things you must possess.

FIRST: WHAT AREAS OF THE STRIKE ZONE YOU HIT BEST

Areas are not the same as pitches. If a backdoor curve, screwball, and rise all arrive in the same location at the same speed, your body timing and barrel position should be the same if you're hunting all those pitches. Having a different approach for the same speeds and locations just adds a layer of complexity to an already hard task.

SECOND: WHAT AREAS YOU DON'T HIT WELL

Unfortunately, this has not been clearly defined for most hitters. When you spend most of your cage and training sessions right down the middle, you never consider evaluating where you're missing.

You've heard this conversation before:

Coach: "How did you hit this weekend?"

You: "I did okay. I went 8-16."

Coach: "Great weekend!"

Four of those hits against someone who will play at a lower level of college than you, who had no horizontal or vertical break exceeding 4 inches. The other hits came off a coach who threw into your barrel. Therefore, you went 0-16 against the pitcher equivalent to your talent. You know, that one that throws 5mph faster than that travel ball pitching. The one that has up to 10" of vertical separation. Or, 16 mph of speed differential. Now, let's discuss the eight hits you didn't get. Are you really ready?

THIRD: HOW DOES YOUR BARREL MISS IN THOSE LOW-PRODUCTIVE AREAS

This element may require a gifted or skilled set of eyes. As previously stated, one of the five is the source of your miss:

Early

Late

Over

Under

Across

Discipline

Proper source identification will keep you from working on a timing solution for a mechanical problem, or a mechanical solution for a timing problem. When your solutions are not correct, this leads to frustration and challenge, especially for those who are intentional about putting in the work.

You've heard it before, right?

"You just have to put in the work"

"You just have to keep working"

"Keep grinding"

Many players are working, unfortunately that time and effort are not directed towards the right solutions.

THE COLLEGE COACH CONSENSUS

After polling a few college coaches from the Power 4 level and asking them what the top challenges are that high school and travel ball players bring with them:

#1: Not understanding their weaknesses and what is required to get better.

#2: Not understanding an approach or game planning. We're talking about some of the best talent in the nation. This should speak volumes to you if you're not one of the most talented players.

The talented player will get a shot prior to the less talented. However, if you have mid-tier talent and an elite approach, timing, barrel position... if you can hit, you can get a chance to play at the highest level of "your" potential.

There are players who are great at hitting given that they just have great hand and eye coordination. That task gets harder as the pitching gets better.

THE GAME CHANGER

A number of college coaches agree on one thing: players don't clearly understand themselves as hitters. This leaves coaches with the task of helping all 20-plus hitters figure themselves out to square the bat up with the ball, and there's more to coaching than just hitting a ball. A player transition game changer is knowing yourself and helping the coaches understand you.

 Think about it: if you walk in the door of your college program able to articulate why you:

"I hit zone 2 and 3 best"

"I struggle zone 7 and 8 with late timing"

"I miss under elevated pitches"

"I need to compensate down-and-in until I correct my path"

"I miss in this area due to timing"

"I miss in this area of the zone due to a specific body position."

You just saved your coach months of trial and error. You just moved yourself up the depth chart.

CHALLENGE #1: THE SELF-KNOWLEDGE AUDIT

Before you arrive at college (or if you're already there), complete this audit:

PART 1: STRENGTHS IDENTIFICATION

Answer with specificity:

What two zones produce my best contact?

What speed range do I time best?

What pitch types do I recognize earliest?

What situations bring out my best performance?

Articulate WHY these are my strengths.

PART 2: WEAKNESS IDENTIFICATION

Answer with honesty:

What two zones produce my weakest contact?

What speed range gives me the most trouble?

What pitch types do I struggle to recognize?

How do I miss in my weak zones? (early/late/over/under/across).

Is the source mechanical, timing, or discipline?

Articulate WHY these are my weaknesses.

PART 3: THE ARTICULATION TEST

Practice explaining yourself to someone (coach, parent, teammate):

Describe your strengths and why they're strengths.

Describe your weaknesses and what's causing them.

Explain what you're working on and why.

Detail your approach and how it connects to your strengths/weaknesses.

If you can't clearly articulate these things, you don't know yourself well enough yet. Knowing yourself is only half the battle...

THE SYSTEM YOU'RE ENTERING

System Of Similarity Vs. System Of Individuality

Unfortunately, most players and families only have the ability to judge a program based on production. That is wins and losses. At the end of the day, the college coach will put a group of players in the lineup that provides the team an opportunity to maximize production. The desired outcome is to maximize runs that will result in maximum season victories. These outcomes will be a byproduct of the coach's preparation in combination with your performance. Your individual growth or productivity will be predicated on the system you're in.

THE TWO SYSTEMS

SYSTEM OF SIMILARITY VS. SYSTEM OF INDIVIDUALITY

The Problem

You have no idea which system you could be entering.

"We develop players"

"We'll maximize your potential"

"We care about individuals."

Table 9.0 - Similarity vs Individuality

Aspect	System of Similarity	System of Individuality
Philosophy	"This is how we do it here."	"What works best for you?"
Approach	Standardized for all	Tailored per player
Strengths	Efficiency, clear messaging	Maximizes individual ability
Weaknesses	Doesn't fit all players	Requires deeper coaching time
Best For	Rigid systems	Player-centered development

When you arrive, you discover:

Everyone swings the same way

Everyone has the same approach

Individual differences are seen as problems to fix

Conformity is valued over optimization.

They told you their truth, it just wasn't your truth.

Or the opposite: you arrive expecting structure and instead get:

Complete individualization with no system

Every player doing their own thing

No accountability or standards

Chaos instead of development.

However, the coach didn't lie. You just had a misconception of how they operated.

The Truth

Some of the most successful programs do a great job of filling a roster with movers and personalities that can fit in their system right away. For those players that transition into a system where individualization is a part of their development, you may be in a better position to thrive versus survive. There is a greater potential of variability here.

Trust me: you will not be the only one with the need for improvement and attention. Think of it like a school. Some schools teach to the test, everyone learns the same way, same pace, same methods. Some students thrive, while others drown.

Other schools teach to the student, different learning styles, different paces, different methods based on need. More students thrive, yet it requires better teachers. Which system fits YOU? Softball and baseball are team sports made up of individual pieces. The key to your journey is to understand who you are, where your opportunities to improve are, and what should be the primary language spoken to you. Even if you're in the right system, you still need to understand something critical...

GAME PLANNING: THE PRACTICE NOBODY HAS

The Approach Assumption

When you understand who you are and pair that up with what the pitcher has, you're more than halfway there. You've possibly been told to "have an approach." I know, I've heard it several times while walking through the park. I rarely hear it in the cage. The problem with speaking it: most never communicate with the player to determine if they know what is meant by having an approach. I often wonder if most who say it know what it means.

The Problem

In my experience with high school to college players, this is an imperative conversation. I must know how they think to tailor my training for them.

The value of a conversation

During a call with a player, I pointed out her vulnerabilities within her swing. There were problems getting in line with the pitch at the top of the zone. Both she and her dad agreed with my in game remote assessment.

The real questions:

Me: "What is your typical approach?"

Her: "Swing at strikes early."

Me: "All strikes?"

Her: "Yes."

Me: "You do agree up and in is a weakness of yours?"

Her: "Yes."

Me: "Well, you know that all strikes are not equal. You just have not incorporated your awareness into your development."

Players have strike zone vulnerability awareness and are still encouraged to "swing at strikes." Oftentimes, this contradiction leaves players confused, and they don't even know it.

The Truth

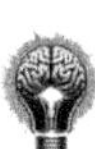 It is easier to identify a hole in a hitter's swing and attack it versus repair it. From a pitching coach's perspective. You spend hours in the cage taking feel good swings without a plan for the weekend. They spend 2 minutes watching your videos to identify what you can't hit. Which is more efficient?

They choose the 2-minute option every time. Which means if you don't have a game plan, they already have one for you. "You call yourself a hunter, yet you are really the prey." What if you could use their weapons against them?

USING TECHNOLOGY TO YOUR ADVANTAGE

The 30-Minute Attack Plan

As I mentioned in Chapter 7, with subscription-based products allowing coaches to watch previous games, there are simple methods they use to establish a plan of attack.

All they have to do is:

Look at where you swing and miss

Identify your weakest contact zones

Identify where you produce power most

Match that with tools each pitcher has

Josh Johnson, while at Mississippi State, informed me he could watch at-bats of a game in less than thirty minutes, all with the purpose of establishing a simple plan of attack. 30 minutes. That's all it takes to build a strategy. His job is easier. Just call the pitch, and hope his pitcher does not miss near the sweet spot.

The Problem

Most players are not equipped to do the same when preparing for the pitcher. You show up to battle, and the other side has: Detailed scouting reports on you, video of at-bats, tendencies charted, weaknesses identified, attack plans prepared.

You have your talent, your confidence, feel good reps, and hope that you'll "figure it out," "I am the best", mindset. It's like showing up to a chess match when your opponent has studied every move you've ever made, and you haven't even looked at the board.

The Truth

Will you become part of a program that equips you to apply some of the same methods pitching coaches will use against you? Those same tools they use for you; you can use for the pitchers. Videos of each pitch during the game can be reviewed, along with a tag. Now, you have to fact-check since some coaches will mistag for those who use these products for scouting purposes. It's as simple as identifying speed and location.

There's one other thing shared with me by Chris Malveaux. The best game preparation includes understanding and giving hitters the look of the pitch. Regardless of location similarities, players see pitches differently. Some need to see the break, some need to know where to be, like Sis, some players can just feel the change up.

The Competitive Advantage

This is where pairing scouting of yourself, understanding how you time, what the pitcher throws, where she throws it, how fast she throws it, and the type of breaks will tilt the scales, giving you a greater advantage over the pitcher. Since pitchers have tendencies and do what they do. As a hitter, you have a greater level of variability. When to start and where to place the barrel. The problem is you have tools in your toolbox, and no one has given you the instructions on how to use them.

The Undervalued Method

One of the most undervalued methods of using this technology is seeing for yourself, through a scouting lens, your strengths and weaknesses. Have a coach show you how they would attack you and why. This could be a great incentive to increase the attention to reduce the size of the holes in your swing.

If you can see yourself the way opposing coaches see you, you can prepare for their attack before it happens. You become proactive instead of reactive.

CHALLENGE #2: THE SCOUTING YOURSELF EXERCISE

This week, become your own scouting department:

PART 1: GATHER YOUR FILM

Collect video from your last 5-10 games (or ask your coach for Synergy/subscription data if available). No excuses. There are complete games on YouTube.

PART 2: CHART YOURSELF LIKE AN OPPONENT

Create a scouting report on yourself: Where do I swing and miss most? What locations produce my weakest contact? What pitch types do I struggle with? What speeds give me trouble? What sequences fool me? What are my tendencies with different counts?

PART 3: BUILD THE ATTACK PLAN

Answer: If I was a pitching coach, how would I attack me? What pitches would I throw? What locations would I target? What sequences would I use? What counts would I exploit?

PART 4: CREATE YOUR COUNTER-STRATEGY

Now that you know their attack plan, prepare your response: What adjustments will I make in practice? What compensations can I use in games? What should my approach be knowing their strategy? How will I force them out of their comfort zone? If you can scout yourself better than they can scout you, you've just gained the advantage. What happens when you don't have time to fix everything?

WHEN TIME ISN'T ON YOUR SIDE

The Correction Vs. Compensation Reality

Having a clear understanding about what hole you have and why you have the hole in your swing can give you answers by compensating instead of answers by correcting movements. Remember from Chapter 6: corrections take time.

They require: Off-season windows, deliberate practice, consistency before stress, trust building. You're in college now. Time is compressed.

You have: Limited practice time, games every week, constant pressure to produce, coaches evaluating every at-bat.

The Problem

Most players try to correct everything in-season. They discover a weakness and immediately try to fix the root cause. Fixing takes time you don't have. So you: Work on corrections during the week, feel uncomfortable in practice, try the new movement in games, fail under pressure, lose confidence, lose playing time, panic and try something else. You're in a death spiral of trying to fix everything and fixing nothing.

Think of it like a surgeon trying to perform a complex operation while the patient is actively bleeding out. Sometimes you don't have time for the ideal solution. You need a fast solution that stops the bleeding.

The Truth

Compensations aren't failures. They're strategic adaptations when time doesn't allow for corrections. Unlike corrections that take time, compensations take a decision. When you arrive at college and discover: Your up-and-in weakness is getting exploited, you don't have the off-season to correct your path, games are starting and you need to produce NOW, you compensate.

You: Adjust your stance to give yourself a better angle, alter your timing to arrive earlier, cheat your barrel position to that zone, hunt speeds that pair with your compensation, step off the plate, get on top of the plate. It's not perfect. It's not pretty. However, it produces.

Production keeps you in the lineup. The lineup gives you opportunities. Opportunities lead to growth. Which is better?

Option A: Try to correct, struggle for 6 weeks, lose playing time, sit on bench, never get another chance.

Option B: Compensate, produce immediately, stay in lineup, earn trust, correct in off-season.

Option B keeps you playing. You can't develop sitting on the bench.

THE FOUR-YEAR WINDOW

Maximizing Your Last Four Years

Let me bring this full circle to where we started: your high school and travel ball success bought you bench time, not playing time. Now you understand: Self-knowledge is your competitive advantage. System fit determines whether you thrive or survive. Game planning levels the playing field. Technology gives you the same weapons they use. Compensation buys you time to make corrections later.

The Problem

Most players waste their first year (or two) because:

They don't understand themselves.

They don't understand the system.

They don't game plan effectively.

They don't use technology available.

They try to correct everything instead of compensating strategically.

By the time they figure it out, they're a junior with limited playing time and limited opportunities to prove themselves. You can't get those years back.

The Truth

You have four years. That's it. Four years to:

Maximize your potential

prove yourself, leave a legacy

Play the sport you love at the highest level you'll ever reach.

After college, for most of you, the game is over. No minor leagues. No professional career. No "I'll figure it out later." This is it.

So the question becomes:

Are you going to spend your four years surviving or thriving?

Are you going to show up hoping your talent is enough?

Or are you going to show up equipped with self-knowledge, strategic game planning, and the ability to adapt faster than your competition?

The Two College Careers

Let me paint you two pictures:

PLAYER A: THE SURVIVOR

Shows up with talent, no self-knowledge. Waits for coaches to figure them out. Has no game plan or approach. Doesn't use technology/scouting. Tries to correct everything in-season. Loses playing time. Sits on the bench. Graduates wondering "what if."

PLAYER B: THE THRIVER

Shows up with talent AND self-knowledge. Articulates strengths and weaknesses clearly. Has detailed game plans for every pitcher. Uses the same scouting tools as coaches. Compensates strategically, corrects in off-season. Earns playing time. Produces consistently. Graduates with no regrets.

Which player are you going to be? The difference isn't talent. Both players have talent. The difference is preparation, self-awareness, and strategic thinking.

CHALLENGE #3: THE FOUR-YEAR MAXIMIZATION PLAN

Before your next season (or before you arrive at college), create your plan:

YEAR 1 GOALS:

Complete Self-Knowledge Audit (Challenge #1). Understand the system I'm entering. Build relationships with coaches. Scout myself (Challenge #2). Identify corrections needed vs. compensations available.

YEAR 2 GOALS:

Make off-season corrections. Refine game planning process. Master technology/scouting tools. Earn consistent playing time. Document growth areas.

YEAR 3 GOALS:

Become a leader who helps younger players. Optimize remaining weaknesses. Maximize production. Prepare for senior year finish.

YEAR 4 GOALS:

Leave legacy. Finish strong. Have zero regrets. Play with freedom.

THE COMMITMENT:

Write down your answers to these questions: What will I do differently after reading this chapter? What advantages do I have that I wasn't using before? What will I stop doing that's been holding me back? How will I measure success beyond stats? What legacy do I want to leave?

THE FINAL TRUTH

Your high school and travel ball success got you in the door. What you do once you're inside determines everything? You can be talented and get lost. You can be prepared and get noticed. You can have four years of frustration. You can have four years of fulfillment. The difference is everything in this chapter.

Self-knowledge. System understanding. Game planning. Technology use. Strategic adaptation. These aren't optional for college success. They're essential.

The coaches already have the advantage. They know you better than you know yourself. They can scout you in 30 minutes. They can build attack plans while you're still figuring out your approach. Now you have the same tools. The question is: Will you use them?

Will you walk onto campus this fall (or walk into practice tomorrow) as a different player? Will you understand yourself? Will you game plan effectively? Will you scout yourself like an opponent? Will you compensate strategically? Or will you keep hoping your talent is enough?

Let me tell you the brutal truth one more time: Your talent got you here. Your preparation will determine if you stay.

You now have the complete roadmap for college success. You understand self-knowledge, system navigation, game planning, technology usage, and strategic adaptation. You have all the tools. Every single one. There's one final barrier that can destroy everything you've learned. One invisible enemy that's more dangerous than mechanical flaws, more limiting than physical weaknesses, more devastating than lack of preparation.

Your beliefs. Right now, somewhere in your mind, there are beliefs about hitting that you've never questioned. Clichés you've accepted as truth. Biases that were planted by well-meaning coaches who never tested whether they actually worked for you. Those beliefs? They're creating barriers you can't even see.

Why do two players with identical talent produce completely different results? Why does one player breakthrough while another plateaus? Why does mechanical correction work for one athlete and destroy another? The difference isn't in their bodies. It's in their beliefs.

In this final chapter, you're going to discover the hidden biases that are holding you back. You're going to learn why "swing at strikes" might be limiting your production. Why "see ball, hit ball" is what coaches say when they don't have answers. Why "just put in the work" is coaching malpractice.

You're going to learn about the two lessons that changed how I coach forever, lessons taught by a player who reminded me that communication is a two-way street, not a one-way delivery system. You're going to face the most important question in this entire book: Are your beliefs creating barriers or breaking through them? This is where everything comes together. Where the 90% from the neck up becomes crystal clear. Where you discover that the cage you're in isn't made of metal, it's made of beliefs.

The key to that cage? It's been in your hand this entire time. You just didn't know to look for it.

CHAPTER 10

HITTING BIASES, BELIEFS and BARRIERS

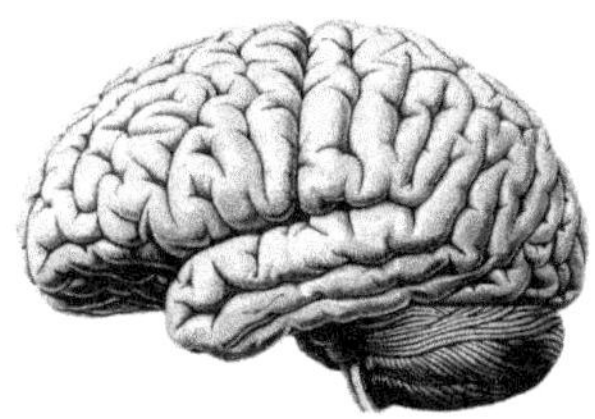

The Sources of Performance Barriers

"The cage you're in isn't made of metal. It's made of beliefs." - Coaching Wisdom

THE INVISIBLE CAGE

You've spent nine chapters learning about:

The three pillars (Decision, Discipline, Damage)

when to trust data and when to trust your eyes

how to assess your strengths and vulnerabilities

the difference between corrections and compensations

how to hunt pitches instead of reacting

the power of expanding your hitting zone

how to maximize your four college years

221

You have all the tools.

There's one final barrier that can destroy everything you've learned. One invisible cage that keeps players imprisoned even when they have the key. Your beliefs. The beliefs that others have planted in you.

THE MIRROR OF BIAS

The Discovery

Personal beliefs can be the source of your present or future performance. I would assume most coaches or instructors apply some level of bias, either consciously or unconsciously. I know I did!

Unconscious bias could be in the way you communicate or teach. I have one buddy who has frequently told me: "Players need to feel it." One day I decided to ask him: "How do you prefer to learn something?" At no surprise, he said: "I learn better when I feel the move or position." Afterwards, I reminded him that there are three main ways of learning: cues, seeing, and feeling. What he just discovered was his personal bias.

The Problem

"What worked for me will work for everyone else." This is the level of bias that a lot of athletes possess when transitioning into coaching. The greater your success, the stronger your personal bias may become. It often takes a while to overcome.

Think of it like a fish that's lived its entire life in saltwater. When it becomes a teacher, it assumes all fish need saltwater to thrive. It never considers that some fish are built for freshwater. The fish isn't trying to harm anyone. It's just teaching what it knows. Consequently, what happens to the freshwater fish in that class? They don't make it.

In my opinion, those who have a growth mindset can remove themselves from unconscious biases. What occurs with a growth mindset is intentional active listening and looking. You look for opportunities to grow. Personally, I'm looking for my wrongs in order to be correct for the athletes.

The Talent Trap

One of the greatest biases that coaches and instructors can encounter is an environment of great talent. Oftentimes, instructors receive too much credit for the God-given talent of the athlete, intensifying the level of bias. Those of us who have had the experience of working with great talent can be honest and say: those special athletes brought more to the table than you possibly could have provided them. Now we take this experience of working with a couple of athletes to validate our biases. As a result, we get rewarded by thinking we know everything about hitting. We don't.

Just like I once was. I didn't know what I didn't know, even when my athletes were having success.

The Truth

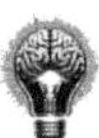 Your coach, your instructor, your mentor, and me, we all have biases. Some biases help you. Some biases hurt you. Sometimes, you won't know which is which until it's too late. Think about medicine. For centuries, doctors believed in bloodletting, draining blood from sick patients. They had success stories. They had theories. They had confidence. They were also killing people.

Not because they were evil. Since their beliefs were wrong, and they never questioned them. Your hitting instruction might be the same. Not evil. Just unquestioned. Unquestioned biases become beliefs.

WHY OUR BIASES GO UNCHALLENGED

Your biases have been protected by silence. Not because they're right. Since no one's willing to call them out. Unless you post it on social media. HaHa! You've been coaching or playing for years with certain beliefs about hitting. Nobody's ever stopped you and said: "Why do you believe that? Where's the evidence? Does it actually work for this player?" Why not?

The Problem

Your biases stay unchallenged for four reasons, and all of them are poisonous:

REASON 1: IGNORANCE The people around you don't have the knowledge to ask the right questions. Think about a parent watching their daughter take a hitting lesson. The instructor says, "Keep your hands inside the ball." Sounds good, right? The parent nods. The player nods. Everyone nods. Nobody asks:

Inside compared to what?

Does that work for her body type?

Is that why she's struggling, or is it something else?

Is that an issue or symptom?

What if the pitch is located higher or lower?

They don't know enough to question it. So, the bias spreads, unchallenged, from instructor to player to team. Like a virus with no immune system to fight it.

REASON 2: FEAR People think you won't listen, so they stay silent. How many times has a parent wanted to question a coach's instruction and didn't? How many times has a player disagreed with their hitting instructor and nodded anyway? Fear keeps biases alive.

Fear of being labeled "difficult"

Fear of losing playing time

Fear of being kicked off the team

Fear of damaging the relationship

So, the bias goes unquestioned. The player suffers in silence. Think about that: your development is being sacrificed to protect someone's ego.

REASON 3: INTIMIDATION Intimidation is used to keep people from asking questions.

"I played at a higher level than you, I know."

"I've been instructing for 13 years. What do you know?"

"If you don't like how I teach, there's the door."

This is the most toxic reason biases survive. Since when questioning equals punishment, nobody questions. Biases become doctrine. Think of it like a dictatorship. The leader's word is law, not as it's right, but because challenging it is dangerous. Your development isn't a dictatorship. It's a partnership, but intimidation turns it into the former.

REASON 4: HERO WORSHIP People assume the subject matter expert (instructor/coach) has all the answers. Here's the belief that kills development:

"They played college ball, so they must know what they're talking about."

"They coached at a high level, so everything they say must be right."

"They're successful, so their methods must work for everyone."

"He coached a WCWS player, he must know."

Wrong. Playing at a high level doesn't automatically make you a great teacher. Coaching successfully doesn't mean your methods work for every player. Having credentials doesn't mean you're always right. Hero worship prevents people from questioning. Since if you believe the expert has all the answers, you'll never ask if their answer is right for you. Think about medicine. A doctor can be brilliant and still prescribe the wrong treatment for your specific condition. Their expertise is valuable, yet it's not infallible. Hitting instruction is the same.

The Truth

Your biases stay alive because:

People don't know enough to challenge them

People are too afraid to challenge them

People are intimidated out of challenging them

People worship them too much to challenge

The result? Players get confined to systems that don't fit them. Talent gets wasted. Potential gets capped. Careers get shortened. All as nobody was brave enough to ask: "Why do we believe this?" What's frightening is that in the era of the transfer portal and NIL, being right by the player has never mattered more. The money you spend can either become a wasted expense, or a wise investment in player development.

The "Tough" Challenge

If you're a coach or instructor, ask yourself:

Do I create an environment where questions are welcomed or punished?

When was the last time I questioned my own biases?

Am I teaching what works for the player, or what worked for me?

Do I intimidate people into silence, even unintentionally?

I have a saying, "It is okay to challenge me, given that I challenged myself first." I make a conscious effort to identify my biases, to eliminate player performance barriers. When we create those barriers, it's really our fault. Unfortunately, the player receives the blame.

If you're a player or parent, ask yourself: Am I staying silent given that I don't know enough, or because I'm afraid? Have I questioned whether this instruction actually fits me? Am I worshiping credentials instead of evaluating results? What would happen if I asked "why" instead of just nodding?

The Final Truth

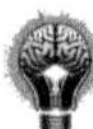

Biases may die when they're challenged or politely questioned. Accepting challenges or questions requires courage. Courage to admit you don't know everything. Courage to ask questions when intimidation is present. Courage to evaluate credentials against results. Courage to separate the expert's success from your needs. Courage to admit you do know now to know later. Do you have that courage? Or will you keep protecting biases that are destroying development? What are some of the most common biases?

THE COMMON HITTING BIASES

The Prison Of Clichés

Let me show you the hitting biases you've heard your entire career. You might even believe some of them right now. For each one, I'll show you the problem, the truth, and the questions nobody asks.

BIAS #1: "DON'T SWING AT CHANGEUPS WITH LESS THAN TWO STRIKES"

WHEN IT APPLIES: This is applicable when you haven't discovered how to hunt the changeup or adjust to the changeup.

THE PROBLEM: In most cases, it appears to be the direction given to the entire team, putting a player or two in a box.

The better coaches will pick up on this and will just steal some free strikes from players who remain disciplined to the "team's" approach.

THE QUESTIONS NOBODY ASKS: Why not teach players to sit on a changeup and be in position to take that pitch away? For those who can, did you just take the bat out of their hands? Have you even taken the time to assess who can sit on changeups and who can't?

THE TRUTH: A team approach might help the majority, yet it creates a prison for the minority who could dominate that pitch. If you can crush changeups, and the team approach says, "don't swing at them," you're being told to ignore your strength?

BIAS #2: "SPREAD OUT AND CHOKE UP WITH TWO STRIKES"

WHEN IT APPLIES: This may not be as drastic of a change for someone who has a wide stance, along with a no-stride or heel-up/heel-down loading pattern.

THE PROBLEM: I'm not sure about this. It appears not to be just an approach change but a swing change. Those with a toe tap or leg lift know you have two different loading patterns in one at-bat if they get to two strikes.

THE QUESTIONS NOBODY ASKS: When changing the loading pattern, will this also change rotational sequencing and connection that will impact barrel path zone entry, especially for those who have a toe tap or leg kick? Are two-strike percentage counts converted over to practice percentages of the reps taken in the cage?

THE TRUTH: You can't practice one timing system and execute a different one under pressure. Think of it like a basketball player who practices shooting one way but is told to shoot differently in games when the score is close. The form breaks down exactly when you need it most.

BIAS #3: "JUST SEE THE BALL AND HIT THE BALL"

WHEN IT APPLIES: This works well for very talented players playing at a level or against a pitcher less than their talent. This approach works when the speed and location pair up well with your natural bat path.

THE PROBLEM: This assumes all pitches are created equal and your natural ability can handle anything.

THE QUESTIONS NOBODY ASKS: Do you just "see" a 2000-rpm rise ball at 66 mph along with a 67 mph drop with 8 inches of drop, along with a 57-mph changeup? If hitting is about "see ball, hit ball," can you hit all these pitches hard? Considering the location is different, which one of these will you have the perfect path for?

The Truth:

> "See ball, hit ball" is what you tell someone when you don't have a better answer. It's not a strategy. It's an abandonment of coaching responsibility.

Think about it: if hitting was that simple, why would anyone struggle?

BIAS #4: "CREATE BACKSPIN"

WHEN IT APPLIES: Well, let's think about this one. There's a tremendous difference in the game of golf and softball/baseball.

That ball on the tee is not moving, and the goal of squaring it up is extremely difficult.

THE PROBLEM: You're being asked to control something that's nearly impossible to control consistently.

THE QUESTIONS NOBODY ASKS: How difficult is it to hit a specific spot on the ball off the batting tee consistently? What about hitting a variety of horizontal and vertical breaks? What about a variety of speeds? What about a variety of locations?

THE TRUTH: "Create backspin" tells you WHAT to do but not HOW to do it. It's like telling someone to "be confident" without explaining how confidence is built.

Or "swing faster" without addressing what creates bat speed. Backspin is an outcome of good path and timing, not a goal to chase.

BIAS #5: "LOOK OUT AND ADJUST IN"

WHEN IT APPLIES: This is a favorite when players are disciplined to this method and I'm calling pitches. When a pitcher can locate on the inner half of the strike zone, it should inevitably become the go-to area for pitchers.

THE PROBLEM: This approach works great until it doesn't. When it doesn't, it creates a massive hole inside or stays away from the sweet spot and closer to the handle.

THE QUESTIONS NOBODY ASKS: How would this work for a player who tends to cast their hands away from their body? What about players who disconnect? Would this create a larger hole in their swing when the pitcher goes inside?

THE TRUTH: You're teaching a weakness. Pitchers will find it. May work for the elite level hitters with tons of at-bats. Are you elite? Think about military strategy: if you always defend the left side and adjust to the right, the enemy will attack the right.

BIAS #6: "JUST PUT IN THE WORK"

WHEN IT APPLIES: Never. This is the laziest form of coaching that exists without specifics!

THE PROBLEM: This is frequently communicated to someone who is struggling. There's a mindset that the time put in will solve the challenges you're facing.

POTENTIALLY: The coach may be satisfied with your progress or production and doesn't want to interfere.

THE QUESTIONS NOBODY ASKS: When you have a timing problem, do you put in the work focusing on mechanics? When you have a mechanical problem, do you focus on timing? If you're having problems at the top of the zone, will you go and work on pitches you prefer only?

THE TRUTH: Working on the wrong thing doesn't fix the right thing. Think about it: if you have a flat tire, does "just put in the work" mean pumping more air into the other three tires? No. You fix the actual problem. "Put in the work" without direction is just wasted effort.

BIAS #7: "YOU JUST HAVE TO FIGURE IT OUT!"

WHEN IT APPLIES: What...

THE PROBLEM: This is what coaches say when they don't have answers and have not provided him or her with any solutions.

THE QUESTIONS NOBODY ASKS: If it's a timing problem, what are we for? If identifying and speaking the player's learning language is needed, what are we for? If it's a mechanical problem, what are we for? If the approach is the problem, what are we for?

THE TRUTH: "Figure it out" is coaching malpractice. If you knew how to figure it out, you wouldn't be struggling. That's literally why you have a coach. Think about hiring a mechanic who says: "Your car won't start. Just figure it out." You'd fire that mechanic.

BIAS #8: "HIT THE BALL THE OTHER WAY" OR "HIT BEHIND THE RUNNER"

WHEN IT APPLIES: We see this frequently with MLB players, and we're talking about the most talented players who may have spent four years in the minors after four years in college.

THE PROBLEM: You're being asked to manipulate barrel location and timing to maximize contact. You inconsistently can maximize contact when you know what's coming. Now you want precise timing and direction.

THE QUESTIONS NOBODY ASKS: How does this work with great velocity inside?

How does this work when your hands work away from your body? Will you have a chance if the inside pitch is thrown and the inner half is your weakness?

THE TRUTH: Manipulation sacrifices contact quality. Contact quality is everything. MLB players can sometimes get away with it as their talent is different. You probably can't.

BIAS #9: "GET YOUR FRONT FOOT DOWN EARLY"

WHEN IT APPLIES: A player is late.

THE PROBLEM: This creates vulnerability to off-speed or change-ups on the outside corner. This creates a reduction in power for your contact hitters.

THE QUESTIONS NOBODY ASKS: Is this a percentage of your cage rounds? Does the player understand their timing trigger?

THE TRUTH: The best cue for this player may be to start sooner. This would allow her/him to maintain their natural rhythm.

BIAS #10: "YOU CAN'T TEACH HITTING"

WHEN IT APPLIES: A player is struggling with consistent contact and the developer has no solution for inconsistent contact and, or power.

THE PROBLEM: The player suffers!

THE QUESTIONS NOBODY ASKS: Has the player timing trigger been determined? Has the natural bat path been identified for the best approach? Have the true sources of the misses been identified?

THE TRUTH: Every player has a best version of him or herself. The question: Are we helping or hindering?

THE CONVERSION PROBLEM

These biases are eventually converted into beliefs. Never tested or discussed. Resulting in performance barriers.

Coaches' barriers, Players beliefs, Performance barriers. How many of these biases do you believe right now? How many have you never questioned? How many are holding you back without you even knowing it?

CHALLENGE #1: THE BIAS AUDIT

This week, examine your beliefs:

PART 1: IDENTIFY YOUR BIASES

Answer honestly: Which of the 5 common biases do I currently believe? Which have I been told but never tested? Which contradict my actual strengths? Which have I passed on to others without questioning?

PART 2: TEST YOUR BIASES

Pick one bias you believe and test it: What evidence do I have that it's true? What evidence contradicts it? Does it apply to me specifically or just generally? Has it helped or hurt my performance?

PART 3: REPLACE OR REFINE

For each bias: Keep it if evidence supports it FOR YOU. Modify it if it partially applies. Eliminate it if it contradicts your strengths. Write down your discoveries. Since unexamined beliefs become performance prisons. The biggest biases don't come from coaches...

THE IMPACT OF BIAS ON PERFORMANCE

The Why Behind The Player

I wonder if we understand the why behind these athletes and the influence we have on their future. Everyone does not have the same why. For those who want to get on the field two or four consecutive years in college, your bias will either contribute to the main goal or contradict it.

The Problem

When we repeat, regurgitate, pass down information we have not fact-checked for the individual, we can be part of the problem. We are the main contributors of the belief this player now has.

If this belief is a performance inhibitor, we are setting this player up to fall short of his/her performance goals. Not the business the athlete is in.

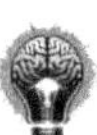

Think about this metaphor: imagine a doctor who prescribes the same medicine to every patient as "it works for most people." Allergic reaction? Not the doctor's problem. Wrong dosage for body type? Not the doctor's concern. Contradictions with other conditions? Doesn't matter. "It works for most people" becomes more important than "what works for YOU." That's what happens when bias overrides individualization.

The Truth

You might be sitting on the bench right now not as you lack talent. Maybe someone's bias is creating your barrier. The worst part? Neither of you know it. You think you're not good enough. They think they're helping you. Both of you are wrong. Let me tell you two stories that changed how I coach forever...

AHMARI LESSON 1: THE IMPORTANCE OF PROCESS

The Expert Trap

I have a saying: We ask athletes to make an adjustment all day. What adjustments are we making? Some of us are the biggest hypocrites. That includes me. In the summer of 2025, Ahmari was playing her second year of summer ball. Like she normally does, prior to reporting for the summer, she comes in to address some of the off-season challenges. Those challenges could range from how she frequently missed the ball to addressing approaches or game planning improvements. On this summer day, I received a video, and the misses were consistent with a few others. I asked

Ahmari to adjust her hand position for a specific reason. Well, she reminded me: "We didn't work on that!"

The Problem

What? "I am the expert! Why won't she just do what I ask? It's only the summertime. She's putting in the work for the spring of 2026!", I thought. All these thoughts went through my mind. After all, she came to me for help, and she is now preventing me from doing my job. I guess I never learned the importance of dialogue with Lana? I was still trying to get her to see things my way, without understanding her beliefs. Think about this: I spent chapter 9 telling you about communication, athlete connectivity, and understanding how players think. I still fell into the expert trap.

The Truth

Ahmari is the type of player that requires confirmation in the cage before competition. This requires: Education (explain why), examples (show how), execution (practice together). In that order. This is how her trust is built. I wanted to skip steps 1-3 and jump straight to game adjustments. Since I was the expert, she should just trust me. Trust isn't automatic. Trust is earned through process.

Think of it like a pilot. Would you trust a pilot who said: "I know you've never seen this maneuver before, but just do it during your next flight"? No. You'd want to practice it in simulation first. Ahmari was asking for the same thing. And I was too biased to see it. I was asking her to make an adjustment, and I wasn't willing to make one myself. It gets worse...

AHMARI LESSON 2: THE POWER OF WORDS

The Productive At-Bat

There was a second occasion where I received a video and immediately provided correction on what was a productive hit. Well, I didn't see the barrel positioning we worked on to produce the consistency for the speed and location we were pursuing. "That is good production, but that may not work against the best pitching in the ACC", I said. Let's say, word got back to me from Mom that I couldn't wait until the summer game was done before criticizing her productive at-bat.

The Problem

My thought was: "You come to me to be the best you can be, and I'm here to do so. If this is my job, she should accept me for who I am!" We're trying to get the best out of her these last two years. Heck, you went from .175 to over .300 in and out of ACC conference play...

"Wait! Rogerick, you're being a hypocrite!" I said to myself. I was biased to my methods of communicating to her. "Isn't it hitting from the neck up? Should you start with the mind and adjust to how she thinks?" I thought. Wow. I caught myself red-handed, not adjusting. One of the biggest ways we can become a hypocrite is expecting the player to make an adjustment and we never make one. Guilty I was.

The Truth

Let me tell you what I discovered. I took a page out of Gary Chapman's The 5 Love Languages. Ahmari has a connection language of words of affirmation. When I criticized her productive outcome, I told her the productive outcome was worthless. The very person that she trusted with her swing crushed her heart.

Some of us have no idea. You're either crushing players' hearts or helping them crush pitches. It's a delicate balance working with these young ladies with big dreams on the line.

The Old Saying Is Wrong

"Sticks and stones may break my bones, but words will never hurt me." Well, they may not hurt you physically, now emotionally they may.

When you hurt them emotionally, you may also be hurting their performance. Now, you may be a reader that doesn't care. Do you care about winning? Do you care about the athlete having a clear mind? This is where you discover the link between instructor bias and performance barrier. They're linked by the biased words and work some players have been inundated with. I am not a coach in this case. I am her hitting teacher. There is time for me to adjust to her. Therefore, I did.

Players must understand coaches are limited with their time and may not be able to accommodate their feelings or learning language. This is the reason it is important to understand your strengths, weaknesses and your language learning before arriving on campus. The ability to communicate these to the coach could be a game changer for you. Here's the deeper lesson...

UNDERSTANDING CONNECTION LANGUAGES

The Three Elements

The link between bias and barrier is the belief that is built in players. Remember what we learned from Ahmari's lessons:

LESSON 1: PROCESS MATTERS

Some players need education, examples, and execution before they trust new movements in competition.

LESSON 2: WORDS MATTER

Some players need affirmation, not just correction. You can crush their heart or help them crush pitches.

The Problem

Most coaches use the same communication style with every player. It's the same tone, same words, same delivery, same expectations.

Players have different connection languages. Some need to feel movements, some need to see demonstrations, some need to hear explanations, some need affirmation, and some need to be challenged.

Using the wrong language creates disconnection, not development. Think about speaking English to someone who only speaks Spanish. It's not that you're a bad teacher or they're a bad student; you just don't speak the same language.

The Truth

Just as coaches have growth mindsets, so do players. You may encounter a player who is in pursuit of becoming the best version of themselves. When they walk through the door, they're bringing their barrier baggage. As you help them unpack, it may be best you start just as the player did as an embryo with the central nervous system, not body parts.

Remember what the only player to ever hit .400 in MLB said? "Hitting is 90% from the neck up." What are the mental and emotional barriers that exist due to the biased environment and personal beliefs? You may discover the majority of a player's challenges have nothing to do with how they move. It has everything to do with how they think. Remember when you discovered the value of time when it comes to offensive production? Now it may be an opportunity to discover the time to understand the player's ways if you want their maximum production.

CHALLENGE #2: THE CONNECTION LANGUAGE DISCOVERY

This week, identify your connection language.

Element 1: HOW DO YOU LEARN BEST?

Rank these learning styles (1-3):

Seeing: I learn best by watching demonstrations.

Hearing: I learn best through verbal explanations and cues.

Feeling: I learn best by feeling the movement in my body.

Element 2: HOW DO YOU RECEIVE FEEDBACK?

What style motivates you most?

Affirmation (Acknowledge what's working, then address needs.) or Challenge (Point out flaws directly, then provide solutions.)

Element 3: COMMUNICATE YOUR LANGUAGE

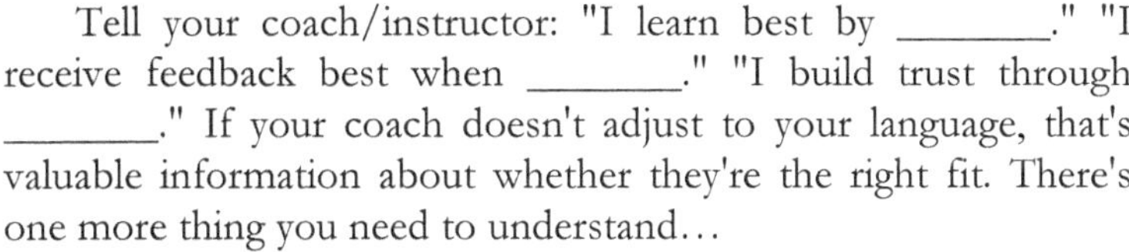

Tell your coach/instructor: "I learn best by _______." "I receive feedback best when _______." "I build trust through _______." If your coach doesn't adjust to your language, that's valuable information about whether they're the right fit. There's one more thing you need to understand…

IT'S REALLY NOT YOUR FAULT OR OURS

The Experience Trap

It's really not our fault if we're not experienced, and some may make you feel inferior as you didn't play at the highest level. Here's what I've learned: you possess two ears and two eyes. I suggest you: Listen with your ears to what is shared, fact-check with your eyes.

The Problem

The industry tells you: "You need to have played at a high level to coach." "If you didn't play professionally, you don't know." "Experience matters more than education." So you doubt yourself. You question whether you're qualified. You let biases go unchallenged as "they played at a higher level than me." Players suffer for it. Some of the best coaches and teachers in MLB, NFL, and NBA never played at the level where they are coaching. Ability to perform and ability to teach are different skills.

The Truth

Your value isn't determined by where you played. It's determined by your willingness to question, learn, and adapt. The best coaches I know question their own biases constantly, test their theories with individuals, listen more than they speak, and adjust to the player. They do not force the player to adjust to them. They also understand that what worked for them might not work for everyone and don't want to be the smartest in the room. That's not about experience. That's about a growth mindset.

THE SOFTWARE APPROACH

Starting From The Beginning

When we start to use our neck up to train players from the neck up, we can create better opportunities for young men and women. Think about how this entire book has been building to this moment:

CHAPTER 1-2: Understanding that hitting is mental (90%) and physical (10%).

CHAPTER 3: The three pillars, Decision, Discipline, Damage, all mental before physical.

CHAPTER 4: Data is only useful when you understand what to look for mentally.

CHAPTER 5: Knowing yourself requires mental self-awareness.

CHAPTER 6: Mechanics serve hitting, not the other way around.

CHAPTER 7: Hunting vs. reacting is a mental distinction.

CHAPTER 8: Discipline to your hitting zone is a mental choice.

CHAPTER 9: College success requires mental preparation.

CHAPTER 10: Biases and beliefs create mental barriers. Everything comes back to the neck up.

The Problem

Most training focuses on: Body positions, mechanical movements, swing paths, physical corrections. The real barriers are: Mental beliefs, emotional connections, biased thinking, unquestioned assumptions. You're trying to fix the body when the problem is in the mind. Think about a computer with a software virus. You can replace the keyboard, upgrade the monitor, and buy a faster processor. The virus remains until you address the software.

The Truth

Just as the player started as an embryo with the central nervous system developing before body parts, your development should start from the neck up, not from the body parts. A talented player with poor beliefs fails. A less talented player with elite mindset succeeds. Two players with identical swings produce different results. Confidence matters more than mechanics. The mind controls the brain, and the brain controls the body. Fix the mind and the body follows.

THE FINAL CHALLENGE

CHALLENGE #3: THE 30-DAY TRANSFORMATION

For the next 30 days, commit to training from the neck up:

WEEK 1: IDENTIFY YOUR BARRIERS

List all biases you currently believe. Identify which came from coaches vs. personal experience. Recognize which help vs. hurt your performance. Write down beliefs that might be limiting you.

WEEK 2: TEST YOUR BELIEFS

Pick your three strongest beliefs about hitting. Find evidence for and against each one. Ask: "Is this true for me specifically?" Eliminate or modify beliefs that don't serve you.

WEEK 3: UNDERSTAND YOUR LANGUAGE

Identify your learning style (see/hear/feel). Identify your feedback preference (affirm/challenge/question). Communicate your language to your coach. Practice receiving information in your language.

WEEK 4: TRAIN THE MIND

Spend 50% of practice time on mental work: Game planning, approach development, self-scouting, timing visualization, use the classroom, allow questions. Spend 50% on physical work: Executing the mental plan, building confidence in decisions, trusting your preparation.

EVALUATION:

After 30 days, answer: Did identifying biases change my performance? Did understanding my connection language improve my development? Did training from the neck up translate to better results? What beliefs am I ready to let go of? What new beliefs will I build?

THE FINAL TRUTH: WHERE WE'VE BEEN, WHERE YOU'RE GOING

The Journey

When you started this book, you probably thought it was about hitting. You thought you'd learn about swing mechanics, bat paths, launch angles, and exit velocity. We did cover those things but what you really learned was hitting is 90% from the neck up.

Everything in this book, every chapter, every story, every lesson, has been building to this realization. Your barriers aren't in your swing. They're in your beliefs.

The Problem

You have spent 90% of your training on the 10%. You've spent hours in the cage perfecting positions. You've taken thousands of swings. You've bought the latest equipment. You've watched countless videos. You haven't examined the beliefs that create your barriers. You haven't questioned the biases that limit your potential. You haven't understood your connection language. You haven't trained your mind as rigorously as your body. And that's why you're stuck.

The Truth

The same players who breakthrough aren't more talented. They're more aware. They know their strengths and weaknesses (Chapter 5), when to correct and when to compensate (Chapter 6), how to hunt instead of react (Chapter 7), their hitting zone vs. strike zone (Chapter 8), how to prepare mentally for college (Chapter 9), which beliefs help and which hurt (Chapter 10). They've done the work from the neck up. When you do the work from the neck up, the body follows.

THE TWO PATHS FORWARD

As we close this book, you're standing at a choice point: **PATH 1: KEEP FOCUSING ON THE 10%** Work endlessly on mechanics, chase perfect swing positions, hope talent is enough, let biases go unquestioned, stay imprisoned by beliefs you've never tested. **PATH 2: COMMIT TO THE 90%** Start with the mind, not the body, question every bias and belief, understand your connection language, train mental skills as rigorously as physical, break free from limitations you didn't know existed.

Most players choose Path 1. It's easier. It's what everyone does. It feels like progress. Path 1 leads to: Plateaus you can't explain, talent that never translates, confidence that disappears under pressure, potential that remains unrealized.

Path 2 is harder. It requires honesty, self-awareness, and questioning everything you've been taught. Path 2 leads to: Breakthrough performance, confidence under pressure, maximized potential, freedom from invisible cages. Which path will you choose?

THE FINAL WORDS

Every player in this book, Lana, Madison, GiGi, Ahmari, Taylar, Hannah Jo, Bryce, and countless others, had talent. Talent wasn't what separated them. What separated them was their willingness to question beliefs, courage to communicate their needs, commitment to training from the neck up, and understanding that hitting is 90% mental.

You have the same opportunity they had. You have the same tools. You have the same knowledge. You have the same choice. Will you use them? Will you examine your biases? Will you test your beliefs? Will you understand your connection language? Will you train from the neck up?

Or will you keep doing what everyone else does and wonder why you're not getting different results?

THE 90/10 PRINCIPLE ONE LAST TIME

Throughout this entire book, we've come back to this again: 90% = Your Mind (Decision, Discipline, Timing, Approach, Beliefs). 10% = Your Body (Mechanics, Positions, Path, Movement). Most players spend 90% of their time on the 10%. Elite players flip that script.

They know the mind is important, though the brain controls the body. They know mechanics matter, but beliefs determine whether mechanics transfer. They know talent is valuable, but mindset determines whether talent gets maximized. This is the secret that's been hidden in plain sight your entire career.

YOUR NEXT MOVE

Write down the three biggest beliefs you have about hitting. Not what you've been told. Not what you think you should believe. What you believe right now.

Where did these beliefs come from? Have I tested them for myself? Do they help or hurt my performance? Am I willing to let them go if they're wrong? Your answers will determine your future. Since the cage you're in isn't made of metal. It's made of beliefs. The key to that cage...

It's been in your hand this entire time. You just didn't know to look for it. Now you do.

ENDING WITH THE BEGINNING

When we start to use our neck up to train the players from the neck up, we create better opportunities for young men and women. This book started with a promise. The promise to make an impact on the sport nationally. The real impact isn't in the mechanics, the data, or the drills. The real impact is in changing how you think about hitting. Hitting is from the neck up. It's always from the neck up. Since hitting, like life, is 90% mental. Are you ready to live in the 90%?

"Hitting is **50**% from the neck up." - Ted Williams, the only player to hit .400 in MLB

Your journey begins now.

A FINAL CHALLENGE FOR COACHES AND INSTRUCTORS

If you're a coach or instructor reading this, I challenge you to ask yourself these questions before your next session with a player. What biases am I bringing? What worked for me that might not work for them? Am I listening or just delivering? Am I adjusting to them, or forcing them to adjust to me? Am I training their mind or just their body?

Then commit to doing one thing differently. Since players are coming to you with dreams, their hearts and futures on the line. They need you to be honest about your biases, willing to question your beliefs, flexible in your approach, and focused on their neck up, not just their mechanics. You either crush their hearts or help them crush balls. Choose wisely.

Your journey is just beginning. Now go train from the neck up.

Use this guide to quickly identify a performance problem, understand its likely source, and locate the chapter where the resolution framework lives. Each card also notes which pillar is primarily involved.

I crush it in the cage but fail in games — *Ch. 1–2*

PILLAR: Decision + Discipline

SIGNS / SYMPTOMS:

- Performs well in batting practice but goes cold against live pitching
- Confidence evaporates when pitcher mixes speeds and locations
- Feels like a completely different hitter in competition
- Stats don't match the effort or the cage performance

RESOLUTION PATH:

- ✔ Understand the hardware vs. software distinction (Ch. 1)
- ✔ Identify whether you have a plan before each at-bat or you are just reacting (Ch.2)
- ✔ Run the PPA Method to assess your actual damage zones (Ch. 2)
- ✔ Install approach principles during off-season, not in-season (Ch. 1)
- ✔ Shift cage work from volume reps to consequence-based rounds (Ch. 2)

I have no plan at the plate — I just react — *Ch. 7*

PILLAR: Decision

SIGNS / SYMPTOMS:

- Steps in the box with vague intent: "swing at strikes," "be aggressive"
- Has no answer when asked what pitch they are hunting
- Gets fooled by speed changes repeatedly in the same at-bat
- Pitchers and pitch callers control every at-bat

RESOLUTION PATH:

- ✔ Build a Pitch Planning Matrix for every pitcher faced (Ch. 7)
- ✔ Learn the difference between acting (hunter) and reacting (reactor) (Ch. 7)
- ✔ Practice naming your hunt zone before every cage rep (Ch. 7)
- ✔ Without pitcher info: monitor catcher location, set rhythm in dugout (Ch. 7)
- ✔ Progress from hunter to sniper only after discipline is established (Ch. 7)

I swing at everything — I have no discipline — *Page 57–88 | Ch. 2, 5 & 8*

PILLAR: Discipline

SIGNS / SYMPTOMS:

- ▸ Chases pitches well outside the zone, especially in high-pressure counts
- ▸ Talent has masked lack of approach at lower competition levels
- ▸ Told to "be aggressive" without being taught when not to swing
- ▸ No framework for what a "good pitch" actually is

RESOLUTION PATH:

- ✔ Define your personal "good pitch" by speed and location, not pitch type (Ch. 5)
- ✔ Run the 50-Pitch Test to confirm actual damage zones (Ch. 5)
- ✔ Implement the Damage Zone Round in practice: 5 pitches, exit on weak contact (Ch. 2)
- ✔ Distinguish between your strike zone and your hitting zone (Ch. 8)
- ✔ Practice the Discipline Round: hunt only, take anything outside zone (Ch. 2)

Two strikes and I fall apart — *Ch. 2, 3, 6 & 8*

PILLAR: Decision + Discipline

SIGNS / SYMPTOMS:

- ▸ Panics with two strikes, becomes mechanical and reactionary
- ▸ Shrinks zone when it may need to expand strategically
- ▸ Loses approach entirely, just trying to "make contact"

> - Goes from hunter to prey in one pitch

RESOLUTION PATH:

✔ Develop a deliberate two-strike approach distinct from your primary approach (Ch. 3, 8)

✔ Identify your two-strike barrel position and timing trigger separately (Ch. 6)

✔ Practice the Bad Umpire Round and Hit-and-Run Round in cage (Ch. 2)

✔ Expand zone strategically, not desperately (Ch. 8)

✔ Understand: two-strike hitting is a trained skill, not a reaction (Ch. 3)

I dominated in high school but struggle at the college level — *Ch. 6 & 9*

PILLAR: Decision + Discipline + Damage

SIGNS / SYMPTOMS:
- High school stats were .400+, college stats are .180–.200
- Weaknesses that were invisible are now being attacked every at-bat
- Pitching coaches know the swing better than the hitter does
- Mechanical adjustments aren't holding under pressure

RESOLUTION PATH:

✔ Accept that high school stats were possibly built on inferior pitch calling or pitching (Ch. 9)

✔ Complete the Self-Knowledge Audit before next season (Ch. 9)

✔ Scout yourself the same way pitching coaches scout you (Ch. 9)

✔ Articulate your strengths and weaknesses to coaches on Day 1 (Ch. 9)

✔ Identify corrections vs. compensations — don't try to fix everything in-season (Ch. 6)

My timing is consistently early or late — *Ch. 6*

PILLAR: Decision

SIGNS / SYMPTOMS:

- Regularly rolling over pitches to the pull side (early timing)
- Consistently getting jammed or missing outside pitches (late timing)
- Can't adjust pitch-to-pitch even when knowing what's coming
- Coach says "be on time" but never explains how

RESOLUTION PATH:

✔ Identify your personal timing trigger: do you time off the pitcher or the ball? (Ch. 6)

✔ Answer the three timing questions: When do you start? What is the start? When do you go forward? (Ch. 6)

✔ Understand that early timing = hunt outside or slower; late timing = hunt inside or faster (Ch. 6)

✔ Address rhythm first before mechanical changes — rhythm disruption causes most timing failures (Ch. 6)

✔ In-game fix: adjust rhythm awareness rather than swing positions (Ch. 6)

I don't know my strengths or vulnerabilities as a hitter
— Ch. 5 & 9

PILLAR: Decision + Discipline

SIGNS / SYMPTOMS:
- Cannot draw personal hot and cold zones on a strike zone chart
- Has never been systematically tested across all zones
- Discovers weaknesses only when pitchers expose them in games
- Describes self as "can hit anything" without evidence

RESOLUTION PATH:

✔ Run the 50-Pitch Test across all six zones: grade A, C, or F (Ch. 5)

✔ Complete the Self-Scouting Report after each of your next three games (Ch. 5)

✔ Complete the Vulnerability Audit, identify the 5 possible miss types (early, late, over, under, across) (Ch. 5)

✔ Know what you do well AND be able to articulate why (Ch. 9)

✔ Spend 70% of practice time in your weakest zone during the off-season (Ch. 5)

My mechanics keep getting "fixed" but nothing improves — *Ch. 1, 4, 6 & 10*

PILLAR: All Three Pillars

SIGNS / SYMPTOMS:

▸ Has received repeated mechanical adjustments across multiple instructors

▸ Each correction creates a new problem or disrupts something that was working

▸ Feels like a different hitter every week

▸ Performance hasn't improved despite technical knowledge increasing

RESOLUTION PATH:

✔ Determine whether the problem is mechanical, timing, or approach-based before touching the swing (Ch. 4)

✔ Ask the Root Cause Assessment Questions before any correction attempt (Ch. 4)

✔ Identify whether a correction or compensation is appropriate for the current timeline (Ch. 6)

✔ Protect what works: if hardware is functional, install software first (Ch. 1)

✔ Audit biases: whose belief system is driving the "fix"? (Ch. 10)

I miss on the same pitch repeatedly and can't self-correct — *Ch.4 & 5*

PILLAR: Decision

SIGNS / SYMPTOMS:

▸ Makes the same mistake in the second at-bat that occurred in the first

▸ Can't identify whether the miss was early, late, over, or under

▸ Blames "bad luck" or "bad swings" rather than diagnosing the pattern

▸ Waits for a coach to tell them what went wrong

RESOLUTION PATH:

✔ Learn the 5 miss types and identify which is most common for you (Ch. 5)

✔ After each at-bat in practice: ask early/late? over/under? across? (Ch. 5)

✔ The Self-Scouting Report: complete for 3 consecutive games (Ch. 5)

✔ Link miss type to the correct solution: timing vs. path vs. discipline (Ch. 4)

✔ Self-diagnosis is the highest form of hitting IQ; train it deliberately (Ch. 5)

I have power in the cage but not in games — *Ch. 3, 4 & 6.*

PILLAR: Damage + Decision

SIGNS / SYMPTOMS:

▸ Exit velocity data looks impressive on grooved pitches, drops in competition

▸ Power disappears when pitcher works the edges or changes speeds

▸ Makes weak contact on pitches that should be power zones

▸ Technology shows strong numbers, but box scores don't match

RESOLUTION PATH:

✔ Distinguish between fancy data (cage) and functional data (game conditions) (Ch. 4)

✔ Run the Cage Reality Check: compare down-the-middle vs. varied locations (Ch. 4)

✔ Address barrel path before exit velocity — path efficiency produces the number (Ch. 6)

✔ Your damage zone is only valuable when paired with the Decision to hunt it (Ch. 3)

✔ Invest in strength and conditioning from coaches who understand rotational athletes (Ch. 3)

I can't adjust mid-at-bat or mid-game — *Ch. 2, 3, 5-7 & 8*

PILLAR: Decision + Discipline

SIGNS / SYMPTOMS:

▸ Same approach in at-bat 1 as in at-bat 4, even after being exploited

▸ Pitchers make no adjustment because they don't need to

▸ Has no "Plan B" when primary hunt isn't available

> ▸ Lacks the slash or compensatory tool when behind in the count

RESOLUTION PATH:

✔ Develop specific adjustment triggers: what changes at 0-2 vs. 1-0 (Ch. 3, 8)

✔ Learn the correction vs. compensation decision framework (Ch. 6)

✔ Study pitcher tendencies between at-bats using the Pitch Planning Matrix (Ch. 7)

✔ Practice the Bad Umpire Round and Hit-and-Run Round to build adaptability (Ch. 2)

✔ Post-at-bat self-assessment: did I make an adjustment? What changes next? (Ch. 5)

My instructor or coach keeps changing my swing and I'm confused — *Ch. 6, 9 & 10*

PILLAR: All Three Pillars

SIGNS / SYMPTOMS:
- ▸ Receives conflicting advice from multiple instructors
- ▸ Never told why a change is being made, just told what to change
- ▸ Trusts credential over evidence and results
- ▸ Feels like they lose their natural movement the more they're coached

RESOLUTION PATH:

✔ Understand biases: instructors teach what worked for them, not necessarily for you (Ch. 10)

✔ Ask why before accepting any correction: "What is the source of the problem?" (Ch. 10)

✔ Identify your connection language and communicate it to your coach (Ch. 10)

✔ Recognize the difference between your system and their system (Ch. 9)

✔ Use the 1,728 Combinations framework to find your natural mechanical pairing (Ch. 6)

I have a great swing but low production — *Ch. 1, 3 & 5*

PILLAR: Decision + Discipline

SIGNS / SYMPTOMS:

- "Pretty swing" that coaches compliment but doesn't show up in box scores
- Hitting .200 with a swing that gets praised in the cage
- Players with "uglier" swings are producing more
- Potential feels unrealized without explanation

RESOLUTION PATH:

- ✔ Accept the core truth: hardware alone cannot solve software problems (Ch. 1)
- ✔ Run the 50-Pitch Test, and identify where actual production exists vs. where it doesn't (Ch. 5)
- ✔ Evaluate approach: do you have a plan, or are you just swinging strikes? (Ch. 3)
- ✔ Invest the same off-season time in software installation as mechanical work (Ch. 1)
- ✔ Review Madison Moak's transformation: .426 / 3 HR to .503 / 16 HR with no swing rebuild (Ch. 1)

My confidence collapses under pressure — *Ch. 1, 5, 7 & 10*

PILLAR: Decision + Discipline

SIGNS / SYMPTOMS:

- Performs differently in practice vs. high-stakes games
- Confidence tied to results rather than to a plan
- Mechanical thinking activates under pressure, further disrupting performance
- No mental framework to fall back on when things go wrong

RESOLUTION PATH:

- ✔ Confidence is a byproduct of clarity, not an attitude to manufacture (Ch. 10 philosophy)
- ✔ Build your plan before the game so the plan becomes the anchor under pressure (Ch. 7)
- ✔ In-season: the mind should only decide one thing, "Is this my pitch, seed and/or location?" (Ch. 1)

> ✔ Identify whether confidence collapses are tied to a specific count, situation, or pitch type (Ch. 5)
>
> ✔ Examine beliefs: are inherited biases creating the mental barrier? (Ch. 10)

CHARACTER APPENDIX

"People are placed in your path to help you grow." The individuals listed here were not actors in a narrative. They were real participants in a decade-plus of research, development, and discovery. Each of them — knowingly or not — contributed to the philosophy in these pages. Their stories are used with respect and gratitude.

Players

Ahmari — *College Softball Player — University of Pittsburgh*

Appears in: Chapters 10

A high-level collegiate player whose two separate cage sessions in the summer of 2025 taught the author two of the most important lessons about coaching: that process matters before application, and that words of affirmation are not optional; they are part of development. Her story closes the book because it reveals the instructor's own biases and the power of communication in player-teacher relationships.

Alana Johnson (Lana) — *Softball — Power 5 Collegiate Player | University of Washington / Texas Tech*

Appears in: Chapters 1, 3, 6, 7, 8

Considered one of the most important developmental examples in the book. Alana began working with the author at age 14. Their decade-long relationship formed the foundation of the Swing Rx philosophy. She earned First Team All-Big 12, Second Team All-Pac 12, and competed in the Women's College World Series in 2023 (Washington) and 2025 (Texas Tech). Her commitment to discipline, her "plate shift" conversations, and her WCWS performances appear across multiple chapters as proof that the approach works at the highest levels of collegiate softball.

Bryce — *Germantown High School Baseball Player*

Appears in: Chapter 3

An exceptionally talented young player whose case demonstrates the Talent Trap; the way natural ability can become a substitute for discipline. His refusal to hold his damage zone in the cage until confronted directly became the teaching example for why discipline is the hardest pillar to develop in highly gifted athletes.

Brooklyn — *Softball — Power 5 Collegiate Player | University of Washington*

Appears in: Chapter 6

A teammate of Alana Johnson's at Washington. Her pre-game conversation before facing NiJaree Canady — the best pitcher in the nation — and subsequent base hit demonstrated how a simple, movement-matched cue can unlock performance in the highest-pressure moments. Her story is the primary teaching example for the compensation concept and for knowing your players' movement patterns before the game requires it.

GiGi — *Softball — High School / Power 5 Commit (Baylor University)*

Appears in: Chapter 6

A Power 5 commit who found herself batting seventh on her own high school team in her senior year. Her in-season breakdown and subsequent rebuild — addressing both mechanical corrections and compensations simultaneously under compressed timeline — is used as the exception-not-the-rule example of in-season correction. She ultimately led her team to a state championship.

Hannah Jo — *Softball — Incoming Power 5 Player (Mississippi State University — 2026)*

Appears in: Chapter 6

A future SEC player who identified and worked on her rise ball vulnerability before arriving on campus. Her story is used as the teaching example for bat path work and for the principle that naming a weakness and confronting it before college is far preferable to being exposed by it freshman year.

Jack (10-Year-Old Pitcher) — *Youth Baseball Player*

Appears in: Chapter 2

The 10-year-old opponent who pitched down and away and exposed the limits of the author's early cage system. Jack didn't know he was teaching a lesson. He just located his pitch. The author's response to being "beaten" by a 10-year-old became the origin of the chalk line, Bad Umpire Round, and the full Three-Round System.

Lauren — *Softball — College Level*

Appears in: Chapter 4

A player the author never coached in person, encountered as an opponent at a tournament in Oxford, MS, where the author was calling pitches against her. Their two-hour phone conversation on the drive home became the origin of Swing Rx's remote development model and the demonstration that the most impactful hitting lesson she ever received happened without stepping foot in a cage.

Lexi Sosa — *Softball — Power 5 Collegiate Player | Mississippi State University (UCLA Transfer)*

Appears in: Chapter 6

An SEC transfer whose rhythm issues were identified in fall ball and confirmed during a conference series against Texas. The author's brief awareness cue, "your rhythm is off, you may be starting too late." led to an immediate home run in the next at-bat. Her story is the primary teaching example for the rhythm concept and the principle that elite players often need awareness, not instruction.

LP — *Softball — High School / JUCO Player*

Appears in: Chapter 1

The player whose 2017 cage session changed the author's entire coaching philosophy. LP was one of the best high school softball players in the state of Mississippi. A single software-based observation. "You're getting your foot down too soon", led to a double off the wall in two at-bats without touching her mechanics. She later became the #3 home run hitter in the nation at the DII JUCO level her freshman season with a .429 batting average. LP's story opens the book's central thesis.

Madison Moak — *Softball — Power 5 Talent (Co-Lin & Nicholls State University)*

Appears in: Chapter 1

A teammate of Alana Johnson's. Madison's year-to-year transformation, a .426 batting average with 3 home runs to .503 with 16 home runs, with only minor hardware adjustment and a focused off-season of software installation is one of the book's most powerful statistical proofs of the 90% principle. She is referenced early in Chapter 1 and cited throughout as the clearest evidence that approach development, not swing rebuilding, drives production gains.

Sam Show — *Softball — Two-Way Player | Oklahoma State University (Professional — Japan)*

Appears in: Chapter 6

Known for the "bat flip heard around the world" at Oklahoma State, Sam Show is one of the most talented players in college softball history. Her appearance in Chapter 6 is not from her college days but from her professional career in Japan, where she reached out to the author for help with consistency. Her willingness to pursue in-season corrections — normally not recommended, and her success in doing so is used as the elite-level exception that proves the correction vs. compensation rule. Her two-way experience gave her the body awareness most hitters never develop.

Coaches, Mentors & Peers

Beth Torina — *Head Coach — LSU Softball*

Appears in: Chapter 5

Asked the author to identify his top three players at an LSU camp without advance notice. The three the author identified were already on Coach Torina's radar. This moment validated that elite coaches see the same things: decision-making, movement efficiency, low vulnerability. That talent assessment at the highest levels is rarely about mechanics.

Boo Ferriss — *Delta State Baseball Coach (Historical Reference)*

Appears in: Acknowledgments / Introduction

The Delta State baseball camp in 1989 run by Coach Ferriss was the author's first introduction to the power of instruction. Referenced as the origin point of the author's passion for the game.

Chris Malveaux — *Hitting Coach (University of Tennessee at the time) / Current – Auburn University Head Coach*

Appears in: Chapters 5 & 9

Shared the insight that "the best game preparation includes giving hitters the look, the feel, and the shape of the expected pitch." This principle elevated the author's understanding of scouting preparation from speed and location awareness to full pitch shape simulation.

Corey Dickerson — *11-Year MLB Veteran / All-Star*

Appears in: Chapters 2 & 7

Validated the 10-year-old hitting approach when he told the author he "didn't understand that concept of hitting until I was a professional." His revelation that MLB players understand discipline and approach in ways most youth instruction never teaches — became one of the most motivating confirmations the author received. Also shared a story of making a real-time in-game compensation based on something he observed in Mike Trout's warm-up.

Corey Ray — *Washington Nationals First Base Coach / Former 1st-Round MLB Pick (5th Overall, 2016)*

Appears in: Foreword (Baseball) & Chapter 7

Wrote the baseball foreword and appears in the MiLB Row 1 story in Chapter 7. At a Double-A game, he was the player who answered "changeup" when asked what he was sitting on, and immediately hit one. His discovery, weeks before that conversation, that his swing was not the problem but his pitch selection was, is used as the professional-level proof of the book's core thesis.

J.T. D'Amico — *University of Washington Softball Staff*

Appears in: Chapter 7

Shared the "two lineup" story that opened Chapter 7. The practice of preparing two different lineups based on which pitcher the opponent started. This conversation permanently changed how the author thinks about player vulnerability and lineup construction.

Jeff Hargar — *Former Arizona State Hitting Coach*

Appears in: Chapter 4

"We measure the body, bat, and ball." These seven words launched the author's exploration of kinematic sequencing and technology-based measurement.

Josh Johnson — *Mississippi State Softball Pitching Coach (Former) / Virgini Tech (Current)*

Appears in: Chapters 9 & 8

Shared that he could build a complete game plan for attacking a hitter in under 30 minutes by watching at-bat video. This revelation became the foundation of the book's argument that players must learn to scout themselves the same way pitching coaches scout them.

Perry Husband — *Discoverer of Effective Velocity*

Appears in: Chapters 3 & 8

The Pitch-A-Palooza napkin conversation that introduced the author to effective velocity — the concept that the same pitch speed is effectively differently based on its location in the zone, is one of the book's most referenced turning points. Perry Husband's research is woven throughout Chapters 3 and 8 as the scientific foundation for why "all strikes are not made equal."

Rodney West — *Travel Ball Coach / Pitch Caller*

Appears in: Chapters 5 & 9

The coach who handed the author the pitch-calling duties against the Prospects, ultimately resulting in a 0–0 tie with 55 pitches thrown in 5 innings. That game became the author's primary example of reading hitters in real time and building an attack plan based on observable swing tendencies.

Samantha Ricketts — *Mississippi State Softball Coach*

Appears in: Chapters 6 & 5

Introduced the author to Lexi Sosa during fall ball at Mississippi State, and provided the bridge between lower-level development and Power 5 competition. Referenced across the fall ball and SEC spring series sections of Chapter 6.

In a one-on-one conversation, Sis shared that she sat on changeups with less than two strikes by feel — "I could just feel it." This answer introduced the concept of timing by feel vs. timing by count, and is used as the example of how elite players develop timing instincts that most instruction never deliberately trains.

GLOSSARY

Acting vs. Reacting

The fundamental distinction between hunters (who act with intent) and reactors (who respond to pitches). Acting involves making decisions before the pitch; reacting means responding after seeing the pitch, which is often too late at higher levels.

Ball Exit Speed (BES)

The speed of the baseball or softball off the bat, measured by technology like Rapsodo or HitTrax. While important, it becomes less useful when collected in cage environments that don't replicate game conditions or competitive at-bats.

Cage Bomb

A ball hit with impressive exit velocity and distance in batting practice or cage work that creates a false sense of hitting ability. The term reflects how these impressive cage hits often fail to translate to game performance.

Cage Star

A player who performs exceptionally well in batting practice but struggles to produce in games. This player typically has strong mechanical skills (hardware) but lacks the mental game (software) needed for game situations.

Damage

The third pillar of hitting, the ability to inflict damage on pitches in your zone. This isn't just about exit velocity; it's about knowing which pitches you can drive and executing when those pitches arrive.

Damage Zone

The specific area of the strike zone where a hitter can do maximum damage, not just make contact, but drive the ball with authority. This zone varies by individual and should be identified through honest self-assessment.

Decision

The first pillar of hitting, the ability to make the right choices about which pitches to swing at and which to take. This involves understanding what you're hunting, recognizing pitches quickly, and making split-second decisions.

Discipline

The second pillar of hitting, the ability to stay within your hitting zone and resist swinging at pitches outside it, even when facing two strikes or pressure situations. This requires mental toughness and trust in your process.

Functional Data

Data collected in conditions that replicate game situations, including competitive at-bats, appropriate pitch speeds, and realistic pitch selection. Contrasts with 'fancy data' collected in non-competitive cage environments.

Hardware

The physical, mechanical aspects of hitting, the swing itself, bat path, timing, rhythm, and body movements. While important, hardware represents only about 10% of what separates good hitters from great hitters.

Hitting Zone

The area where you can consistently do damage, different from the strike zone. Your hitting zone should be smaller than the strike zone and represent pitches you can drive, not just contact.

Hunter vs. Reactor

Hunters have a specific plan for each at-bat and actively look for their pitch, while reactors wait to see what comes and then respond. Hunters gain time and advantage; reactors are always behind in the count.

PPA Method

Pen, Paper, Arithmetic, a simple, low-tech assessment system for collecting functional hitting data. Uses basic tools to track meaningful metrics like decision-making, discipline, and damage rather than relying on expensive technology.

Pitch Planning Matrix

A strategic framework for planning your approach to each at-bat based on count, pitcher tendencies, and your strengths. Helps hunters develop specific plans rather than reacting to pitches.

Software

The mental aspects of hitting, decision-making, discipline, pitch recognition, approach, and the ability to execute a plan. According to Ted Williams, this represents 50% of what separates elite hitters from the rest. In today's time or in season, up to 90%.

Strike Zone Prison

The limiting belief that you must swing at all strikes and can't swing at balls, which prevents hitters from developing discipline to their actual hitting zone and expanding strategically when beneficial.

The Three Pillars

Decision, Discipline, and Damage are the three essential mental elements that every collegiate and elite hitter possesses. These pillars work together: good decisions about what to hunt, discipline to wait for it, and damage when you get it.

INDEX